CW00537078

S·H·P

THE
SCHOOLS
HISTORY
PROJECT

# DISCOVERING THE PAST Y9

# PEACE &WAR

# TEACHERS' RESOURCE BOOK

## SECOND EDITION FOR THE REVISED NATIONAL CURRICULUM

*Colin Shephard (Director, SHP),*
*Andy Reid and Keith Shephard*

**JOHN MURRAY**

**Acknowledgements**

The authors and publishers are grateful to the following for
permission to reproduce copyright material:
Transworld Publishers Ltd. for *The Past is Myself* by Christabel
Bielenberg; Victor Gollancz for *Carrie's War* by Nina Bawden; and
to the following for permission to use copyright illustrations:
**p. 56** Glamorgan Archive Service; **p. 58** East Sussex County
Library; **p. 61** Oxford City Library; **p. 62** *top* Mary Evans Picture
Library; *bottom* Janet and Colin Bord/Barnaby's Picture Library;
**p. 72** *top* Tate Gallery, London/Bridgeman Art Library;
*bottom* A. F. Kersting; **p. 77** *Evening Standard*/Solo;
**pp. 116–117** D. C. Thomson.

Every effort has been made to trace all the copyright holders, but
if any have inadvertently been overlooked, the publishers will be
pleased to make the necessary arrangement at the first
opportunity.

**Note:** The wording and sentence structure of some written
sources have been adapted and simplified to make them accessible
to all pupils, while faithfully preserving the sense of the original.

**Pupils' Book** ISBN 0–7195–4977–9
**Teachers' Resource Book** ISBN 0–7195–7042-5

© Colin Shephard, Andy Reid, Keith Shephard, 1993, 1995

First published 1993
by John Murray (Publishers) Ltd
50 Albemarle Street
London W1X 4BD

Second edition 1995

Reprinted 1997

Illustrations by David Anstey and Art Construction

Layouts by Amanda Hawkes
Printed in Great Britain by St Edmundsbury Press,
Bury St Edmunds

A CIP catalogue record for this book is available from the
British Library

ISBN 0–7195–7042-5

# Contents

## Introduction

## Teachers' notes and worksheets

### Britain 1750–1900

### The Twentieth-Century World

# Introduction

## About the series

### *Discovering the Past* Series Editor
Colin Shephard (Director, Schools History Project)

*Discovering the Past* is SHP's integrated series of full-colour course books and teachers' materials for NC History – for all Key Stages.

### ■ Coherence in Key Stage 3
The core texts combine statutory units and SHP-designed approaches to the European and non-European units into a coherent course for each year. In Y9, for instance, the course deepens pupils' understanding of causation, through an extended analysis of the causes and consequences of the Industrial Revolution, in Unit A (Britain 1750–1900), and of the causes and consequences of the Second World War, in Unit B (The Twentieth-Century World). Alternative supplementary study units, such as *The Changing Role of Women*, allow schools to follow a range of pathways without losing that coherence.

Please note that we have used the new unit titles throughout this book – Britain 1750–1900 and The Twentieth-Century World in place of Expansion, Trade and Industry and The Era of the Second World War.

### ■ Planning across the Key Stage
By planning across each Key Stage, we have been able to cover comprehensively the overall requirements for the Key Stage by, for example:

— selecting a range of case studies to reflect the social, cultural, religious and ethnic diversity of society: this means covering the varied experiences of both women and men, and both rich and poor, throughout the course, and covering controversial topics from a range of perspectives, e.g. in Y7 seeing the Crusades through both Islamic and Western eyes
— developing pupils' understanding of the key terms for Key Stage 3, which range from feudalism to Fascism and from revolution to dictatorship
— offering clear opportunities for pupils to trace developments in Britain over the period of the statutory units, from 1066 to the twentieth century.

### ■ An issue-based approach
Issues and questions raised by the content give each unit its identity. These genuine historical issues and controversies encourage pupils to question conventional interpretations of the past.

### ■ The role of the individual
By focusing on case studies of particular places and individuals, the series avoids historical stereotypes. Instead, pupils can begin to appreciate the variety and complexity of a period.

### ■ Classroom appeal
The series uses the best classroom practices, combining innovation and familiar techniques to ensure variety for the pupil and the teacher. A range of readers, advisers and (in Key Stages 1 and 2) trialling schools have ensured the classroom appeal of the material across the Key Stages.

### ■ Special Needs Support
Special Needs Support Material is available or is in preparation for each of the statutory units in Key Stage 3 (see page 126 for details).

### ■ Source-based activities
The pupil tasks and enquiries use a wide range of source material — so that source-based work is thoroughly integrated into work on historical understanding.

### ■ Enquiry and communication
The series offers a wide range of exercises that allow pupils to present their historical findings in extended writing, using a variety of techniques such as reports, essays, diaries, leaflets, letters or articles.

### ■ Assessment and the Attainment Target
Enquiry-based pupil tasks and questions are provided throughout to help pupils of all abilities progress in History.

The series is built on SHP's considerable assessment expertise. Guidance on teacher-based assessment at the end of Key Stage 3 is provided.

## THE SCHOOLS HISTORY PROJECT

This project was set up by the Schools Council in 1972. Its main aim was to suggest suitable objectives for history teachers, and to promote the use of appropriate materials and teaching methods for their realisation. This involved a reconsideration of the nature of History and its relevance in secondary schools, the design of a syllabus framework which shows the uses of History in the teaching of adolescents, and the setting up of appropriate examinations.

Since 1978 the project has been based at Trinity and All Saints' College, Leeds. It is now self-funding and with the advent of the National Curriculum it has expanded its publications to provide courses throughout Key Stages 1–3, and for a range of GCSE and A level syllabuses. The project provides INSET for all aspects of National Curriculum, GCSE and A level history, and also publishes *Discoveries*, a twice-yearly journal for History teachers.

Enquiries about the project, INSET and *Discoveries* should be addressed to the Schools History Project, Trinity and All Saints' College, Brownberrie Lane, Horsforth, Leeds LS18 5HD.

Enquiries about the *Discovering the Past* series should be addressed to the publishers, John Murray.

### Series consultants
Terry Fiehn
Tim Lomas
Martin and Jenny Tucker

# Peace and War

## ABOUT THE PUPILS' BOOK

■ The main aim of this course is to help pupils realise how fascinating History can be. The course is founded on a belief that thirteen- and fourteen-year-olds can cope with an investigation of real historical issues – issues that would interest a historian – if they are presented at an appropriate level.

The two units in *Peace and War* have seen the greatest changes under the revised curriculum. However, the content, structure and approach of the book remain as valid as ever.

■ The statutory content for Unit 3, **Britain 1750–1900** and Unit 4, **The Twentieth-Century World** has been covered. This has been done through the use of enquiries – discrete pieces of work on discrete themes – rather than by slavishly following the list of topics in the Programme of Study.

In Britain 1750–1900, for example, there is no separate section on 'the growth of trade and Empire'. Instead, this is tackled through enquiries on the slave trade, the causes of the Industrial Revolution, the growth of Brighton, the nature of Victorian values, eighteenth- and nineteenth-century racism, and London, the imperial capital.

Similarly, in The Twentieth-Century World, there is no single section on 'the consequences of the First World War'. Instead, this is handled through enquiries on the Treaty of Versailles, the rise of the dictators, Appeasement, the League of Nations, and American isolationism.

The panels on pages 6–7 and 8–9 summarise how the statutory requirements of each unit have been covered.

The panels also illustrate how opportunities for depth study have been provided throughout the book, and how regular overviews of the entire unit, and of themes within each unit, are tackled. Our approach to depth studies and overviews is explained on page 4 of this book.

■ Both units contain topics which Y9 pupils can find difficult to grasp: 'causes of the Second World War', for example. We have attempted, therefore, to give pupils a clear structure, in this case looking first of all at the causes to do with individuals (*Hitler's War*), then moving on to more impersonal causes in case studies of such subjects as the Treaty of Versailles or the policy of Appeasement.

Likewise, we have taken the view that the best way to examine 'industrialisation' is to focus on a few selected case studies of places and events, rather than by trying to cover the whole subject in a superficial and general way.

Throughout the book, however, we have supplemented the depth study approach with clear and compact 'survey' spreads, which allow pupils to see the case study in its broad context.

■ The new NC order strongly encourages pupils to investigate links between units. The books in the Discovering the Past series have encouraged such links from their first publication – as the book titles *Contrasts and Connections*, *Societies in Change* and *Peace and War* amply illustrate.

In each book many opportunities have been provided for making links and connections. In *Contrasts and Connections*, for example, there are comparisons between life, practices and beliefs in medieval England and those in the Islamic world at a similar time; in *Societies in Change*, one of the comparisons drawn is that between Louis XVI and Charles I.

The two units in *Peace and War* might appear to have very different focuses. However, there are clear links between them. Unit A, for example, helps to establish pupils' understanding of some of the key ideas needed to study Unit B – such as Empire and democracy.

There is also a very clear conceptual link to do with pupils' understanding of causation. The first sections of Britain 1750–1900 form an extended investigation of the causes of the Industrial Revolution, while the first part of The Twentieth-Century World investigates the causes of the Second World War. The two units are designed to provide progression through the year; by the end of Y9 pupils should better appreciate the dynamics of cause and consequence. They should see how causal explanations are, by their very nature, complex and varied.

■ On pages 14–18 we explain in detail how this book meets the requirements of the Key Elements and the Attainment Target. However, the course has been neither assessment led nor AT led. Rather, the aim has been to provide real historical questions and activities that are worthwhile in their own right and create learning opportunities for the pupils. The majority of these questions and activities are to be used simply to increase pupils' historical knowledge, understanding and skill, rather than for assessment purposes.

Furthermore, the aim has been to design the questions and activities to be genuinely accessible by all abilities. We have allowed for differentiation by outcome rather than by task, while using the detailed notes and worksheets in this Teachers' Book to highlight occasions when support may be necessary for some pupils. There is further guidance on this subject on page 11. Special Needs Support Materials are in preparation for both units (see page 126).

■ Finally, we have aimed to help pupils to learn how to do the work of the historian: to organise their historical ideas and findings, to ask their own questions, to collect and record information, and to present their results using a range of different techniques.

The book is based on issues and enquiries to encourage pupils to reach their own conclusions and to question stereotypical views of the past. Care has been taken to provide information about each enquiry in sufficient depth to allow pupils to base their conclusions on full and sound evidence.

It is very important that pupils produce some history of their own, and construct their own view of the past.

The major activities at the end of each enquiry throughout the book are geared to this fundamental objective.

## ABOUT THE SECOND EDITION OF THE TEACHERS' RESOURCE BOOK

The revised National Curriculum which came into force in September 1995 has underlined the importance of many features adopted by *Peace and War*: the pursuit of real historical questions rather than statement of attainment targeted work; the study of selected aspects of history in depth, others in overview; the integration of source-based work with work towards other historical understanding; and, most notably, the emphasis on giving pupils opportunities to tackle some major pieces of historical investigation – through which they can display their knowledge, understanding and skill.

There have therefore been no changes made to the Pupils' Book, as we believe the learning objectives, the methodologies and the content coverage remain more valid than ever under the revised curriculum.

However, this Teachers' Resource Book has been revised to reflect the following aspects of the new order:
(a) that both Y9 units are now structured as overview plus depth studies
(b) that the three ATs have been conflated into one, and the statements of attainment have been lost
(c) that the Programme of Study, including the Key Elements, has become a more major planning tool than the AT
(d) that the trimming of the statutory core has opened up the possibility of tackling some areas of the units in much greater depth than could be done previously.

At the same time, the second edition has given us the opportunity to learn from the experience of three years' use of the Pupils' Book and to provide some additional teaching notes and worksheets.

## PEACE AND WAR IN THE REVISED Y9 CURRICULUM

*Peace and War* provides a coherent and comprehensive course for Y9 under the revised curriculum, although you might need to replan your teaching pathways through the book.

Experience of teaching Key Stage 3 has clearly shown that the selection of content within study units is crucial in determining whether or not your Key Stage 3 course is successful. In particular those teachers who have attempted to use a study unit outline as a teaching scheme and have tried to teach all the prescribed topics in the same depth have often found themselves rushing through topics in a superficial way and failing to stimulate pupils' interest.

Indeed this problem has been widely recognised and is one of the reasons why the revised National Curriculum and the new orders have called for more selective treatment of content. The new order requires that:

a) **throughout the Key Stage** pupils should be given opportunities to study some aspects of the past in outline and some in depth
b) **Units 3 and 4** have to be covered through an overview of the main events, personalities and developments, and through a depth study of at least one aspect of the period.

As we explain in detail below, this approach – combining depth studies with overviews – is already central to the organisation of *Peace and War*, as it is to the entire Key Stage 3 series.

### Depth studies

All the books in the *Discovering the Past* series were designed to provide studies in depth for pupils. Throughout the series we have deliberately concentrated on certain aspects of each unit at the expense of others. We included a wide range of depth studies so that teachers had a wide choice of content and approach. As a result teachers have been able to choose pathways through our books which best serve to inspire and motivate their pupils and, equally importantly, to interest the teaching staff themselves.

As you will see from pages 6–9, this continues to be the case – *Peace and War* provides an abundant range of stimulating and engaging depth studies.

### Overviews

The overview requirement in Key Stage 3 History is not an innovation. A well-constructed History course has always included scene-setting overviews which allow pupils to put whatever they are studying into a wider context.

Several devices are used in *Peace and War* to help you achieve this overview of the units (see pages 6 and 8).

There are no firm rules as to how long or detailed an overview has to be, how it should be used, nor whether it is undertaken at the beginning, in the middle, or at the end of a unit. It can be useful to conduct several overviews, at different times, each on a different aspect of the unit (as we have done in both units of *Peace and War*).

However, one thing is critical – that overviews do not develop into an eight-week trot through the entire unit. Too much detail in an overview confuses pupils. Overviews should be brief and clear. **Remember that the main aim of the overview is to provide your pupils with an overall sense of the shape of the period, or a bird's-eye view of the main developments**.

### Key questions

One other defining feature of the series is the use of key questions. This approach to organising historical enquiry was pioneered by SHP and has now been widely adopted elsewhere. Its advantages become particularly clear when you are required to integrate coverage of the overview and depth-study content of the units with coverage of the Key Elements.

By asking key questions such as 'Why was slavery abolished?' (pages 82–85) or 'Was the Treaty of Versailles a mistake?'(pages 116–117 and 136–137) several things are accomplished at once:

■ The statutory content of the units is reorganised into investigations which encourage and allow work in depth

■ Pupils are given the opportunity to carry out an investigation, reach their own conclusions, and organise and communicate their findings

■ All aspects of the Key Elements and the Attainment Target are covered, but in a natural and unobtrusive way. (The subject of the coverage of the Key Elements and the Attainment Target is discussed in detail on pages 14–18).

# STUDY UNIT 3  BRITAIN 1750–1900

The Programme of Study/Content requires that pupils should:

**1.** find out about in overview:

**Britain's worldwide expansion**
**(a)** the growth of trade and the Empire and its impact on Britain and the colonies

**Industrialisation**
**(b)** industrial change and its impact on the way of life of people at different levels of society

**Political developments**
**(c)** the influence of personalities and events, including the American Revolution, French Revolution and the Napoleonic Wars, the extension of the franchise, popular protest and reform.

**2.** undertake a study in depth of at least one of the main events, personalities or developments and its significance.

## A POSSIBLE APPROACH TO THIS UNIT USING PEACE AND WAR

### 1 (a)–(c)  Overview
There are a range of possibilities open to you:
■ The opening spreads of Britain 1750–1900 provide an opportunity for pupils to consider how different things were in 1750, 1825 and 1900. These pages give a simple and accessible overview of some of the main changes and help pupils begin to develop a feel for the period.

This could be the only overview you attempt. It raises issues to return to when pupils are working on their depth studies, and at the end of the unit.
■ Pages 40–41 provide an overview of the main changes in transport.
■ Pages 42–45 provide an overview of the growth of trade and Empire.
■ Pages 50–51 use the true stories of two families to provide an overview of the period at a personal level.

This helps to show how the changes taking place in this period affected real people. The enquiry shows changes in different areas of life coming together, and questions some of the stereotypes often found in textbooks.
■ Pages 86–87 contrast the political system in the 1820s with that in the 1990s, providing another useful overview to show how much has changed, while pages 100–101 summarise the story of popular protest over the period and encourage pupils to detect patterns in this story.

Any of these overviews from *Peace and War* could be used if you are not using a depth study from that particular subject area, or they could be used to put a depth study into a broader context.

### 2.  Depth Studies
The number of depth studies you tackle, and their length, is entirely up to you, the teacher.

Given the increased time available for each unit, and provided that you spend just a couple of weeks on an introductory overview, there should be time for two or three studies in depth.

These should be selected to cover a range of perspectives (social, political, economic, etc.), and should vary in type, to include, for example:
■ a study of an individual
■ a study of one place
■ a study of a development over time
■ a study of a significant event.

Unit A of *Peace and War* has been written as a series of depth studies. The section headings indicate the focus –
- *What made British business tick?* (pages 8–23)
- *What caused the Industrial Revolution?* (pages 26–49)
- *Was life getting better?* (pages 50–61)
- *Victorian values* (pages 64–81)
- *How did people bring about change?* (pages 82–101).

Any of these sections could form your 'depth study'.

However, there are also plentiful opportunities for teachers to develop different depth studies which are tailored to the interests of their pupils, by combining different parts of the book.

The following depth studies could then emerge:

**(a)** The development of British industry (using pages 8–15 and 22–25), focusing on the case studies of the Darbys, Arkwright, and Boulton and Watt.

**(b)** Changes in the countryside, including a case study of the village of Ashill (using pages 26–29 and 52–55).

**(c)** Changes in transport, including a case study of the Liverpool-Manchester area (the Bridgewater Canal and the Liverpool and Manchester Railway; using pages 32–39).

**(d)** The slave trade, slavery and its abolition (using pages 42–44, 70–75 and 82–85), including an examination of conditions on slave ships, slavery on the sugar plantations, the experience of black people in Britain and the campaign to abolish slavery.

**(e)** Working conditions and attempts to improve them (using pages 16–21 and 80–81), including an examination in particular of the experiences of women and children in factories and mines, the ideas and practice of Robert Owen and other reformers.

**(f)** Changes in living conditions (using pages 56–59), based around a case study of the industrial town of Merthyr Tydfil.

**(g)** The development of seaside resorts (using pages 60–63), in particular a case study of Brighton.

**(h)** Victorian values (using pages 64–81). This involves a study of a range of Victorian attitudes towards, for example, black people and slavery, the poor and women.

**(i)** Electoral reform and its consequences (pages 86–95), including the struggle for change in 1832 and the Chartists.

**(j)** Popular protest (pages 82–85 and 90–99), looking at popular campaigns for electoral reform, abolition of the slave trade, better working conditions, etc.

**(k)** Was the nineteenth century a turning point for women? This depth study would begin on pages 80–81 of *Peace and War*, then continue with the separate publication *The Changing Role of Women*.

There is also sufficient material for smaller-scale studies of significant individuals, such as the Darbys, Joseph Arkwright, Robert Owen, Matthew Boulton, Thomas Coke, James Brindley, Robert Stephenson, Olaudah Equiano and Annie Besant.

It is important to make a balanced selection from this list, aiming for a reasonably even coverage of the Key Elements, looking at history from a range of perspectives, but above all keeping in mind the interests of your pupils.

## Special Needs Support for Britain 1750–1900

Our recently developed Special Needs Support Materials for pupils with learning difficulties are based around an overview and the following depth studies (from which we envisage you might choose two or three):

**(a)** Women and children at work
**(b)** Changes in transport
**(c)** Black people in Britain
**(d)** The story of two families
**(e)** Ashill: what changed in the country
**(f)** The workhouses: the story of Harriet Kettle
**(g)** Trying to get the vote

# STUDY UNIT 4  THE TWENTIETH-CENTURY WORLD

The Programme of Study/Content requires that pupils should:

**1.** find out about in overview:

**(a)** the First World War and its consequences.

**(b)** the Second World War, including the Holocaust and the dropping of the atomic bombs.

**(c)** the legacy of the Second World War for Britain and the world.

**2.** undertake a depth study of at least one of the main events, developments or personalities and its significance.

## AN APPROACH TO THIS UNIT USING PEACE AND WAR

### 1. The overview

This is obviously a complex period and pupils of this age can have difficulty making sense of it.

It is therefore worth emphasising the point again that overviews which are clogged up with too much detail will not help pupils to form an overall sense of the shape of the period.

You may decide that the accessible material for pupils of this age range is to be found in a depth study of aspects of the First and Second World Wars rather than in the international events of 1919–1939 which could be covered with an overview.

These are some of the options available to you for covering the period in overview:

■ The timeline on pages 108–109 could be used to establish some of the important events of the period.

A large copy of this on the classroom wall could then be regularly referred to and could be illustrated with pupils' work.

■ Use pages 114–115 to give an overview of the First World War for those who are not tackling this subject in depth.

■ Pages 148–149 provide an accessible survey of the years 1919–1939 and the main events leading to war for those teachers who decide to cover this period by overview only.

They can also be used to reinforce and clarify more detailed work on the period.

■ Pages 150–151 provide a summary of the main events of the Second World War.

It is clearly not possible to cover all aspects of the war in detail and most teachers will concentrate on certain aspects for work in depth.

An overview such as this one is therefore necessary to provide the context for the depth studies.

■ Pages 208–209 provide an overview of another complex topic – the relationship between the allies from 1941 to 1948.

### 2. Depth studies

Our coverage of this unit is already structured as a series of studies in depth as the list of key questions and enquiries demonstrates.

However, it is important to remember that there are many other ways of organising the material in the book to provide alternative depth studies of shorter or longer length.

The following depth studies could then emerge:

**(a)** Who was to blame for the First World War and should Germany have been punished in 1919? (pages 110–117 and 136–137).

**(b)** The First World War. If you wish to tackle this in depth you will need our parallel publication *Britain and the Great War* which includes depth studies of various aspects of the war including *The Home Front*, *The Western Front*, and *Was the war a turning point for women?*

**(c)** The dictators (pages 118–123): a comparative study of Stalin, Mussolini and Hitler, followed by a particular focus on Hitler (pages 120–131, 203 and 205), covering his domestic and foreign policies, and his role as a wartime leader.

**(d)** The Home Front in the Second World War (Pages 152–157 and 164–171) or more focused studies on Evacuation (pages 152–157) and the Blitz (pages 164–169). The case studies in *Experiences of war* (pages 182–185) could be contrasted with life on the Home Front in Britain.

**(e)** A number of key military incidents in the war can each be studied in depth or form part of an extended study of the events of the war: Dunkirk (pages 158–161); the Battle of Britain (pages 162–163); the Eastern Front including the siege of Leningrad (pages 172–175); the Battle of the Atlantic (Pages 176–179); Pearl Harbor (pages 180–181).

**(f)** The Holocaust (pages 186–193) is studied in depth, with particular emphasis on putting the events against the historical background of anti-semitism; and painting as full a picture as possible of the response of the Jews – including attempted resistance.

**(g)** War crimes: what was and was not a war crime? (pages 186–201). This idea is explored in greater detail on pages 89–90 of this Teachers' Resource Book and additional worksheet support is also provided, allowing for comparisons of the bombing of Dresden (pages 194–197), the use of the atomic bomb (pages 198–201) and the Holocaust, in the context of war crimes. The Battle of the Atlantic is also investigated in the same context.

**(h)** The beginnings of the Cold War (pages 206–211).

**(i)** The United Nations and the Universal Declaration of Human Rights (pages 212–213) including comparisons with the League of Nations (pages 142–145).

There is also scope to investigate the role of the following individuals: Hitler, Churchill, Stalin and Roosevelt.

## Special Needs Support for the Twentieth-Century World

Our recently developed Special Needs Support Materials for pupils with learning difficulties are based around an overview and the following major depth studies:

**(a)** The Trenches: the Western Front in the First World War

**(b)** The Home Front in the Second World War with additional support material on the other depth studies in the list above.

There are other ways of using this freedom of choice between enquiries. On occasions you might wish to use different enquiries with different classes, or even different groups in a class. For example, each group could study one aspect of the Industrial Revolution (from pages 26–49), or one cause of the Second World War (from pages 118–147), and at the end of their one- or two-week project make a presentation to the rest of the class. More importantly, the groups can also select or devise tasks that they regard as important for the rest of the class to tackle. The class as a whole could then continue by comparing the relative importance of the features each group has studied.

This also has the advantage of involving pupils in the choices governing what they learn and how they learn. Listening to pupils' own questions, offering a choice of task and allowing them to pursue their own favoured line of enquiry will all help increase motivation.

## HOW TO USE THIS BOOK

We are assuming that most schools will give approximately a term's teaching to each unit in *Peace and War*. Each unit has a separate set of notes in this book, but links between the units are picked up as they arise.

Each unit of the Pupils' Book is split into a number of *enquiries*. The enquiry is a discrete piece of work on a discrete theme. Each enquiry covers one, two, three or four double-page spreads in the Pupils' Book.

There is usually enough in an enquiry to keep a class busy for a number of weeks, with or without homework. However, schools spend such varying amounts of time on History that we have had to build in a great deal of flexibility. We have already explained above how you might select enquiries to provide for your overview and depth study requirements in Y9.

In each enquiry there are questions to be done en route. These appear in yellow boxes. For convenience, the questions normally return to number 1 after a new subheading.

At the end of the enquiry, in a blue box, there is usually a major piece of work bringing together themes from the previous few spreads. The questions and discussions during the rest of the enquiry are an important part of the process of getting ready to answer these summary questions.

The main purpose of the summary questions is to show how pupils have brought together a range of skills and understanding. However, they are also crucial for harnessing pupil motivation. Pupils like to have something to show for the work they have done in History, and the summary questions and activities are designed to achieve this.

The enquiry is also the basis for the organisation of the detailed teaching notes which begin on page 22 of this book. For each enquiry there is:

■ a brief description or statement of purpose
■ detailed guidance on how to introduce a topic
■ additional background information for teachers
■ suggestions on which questions to use for discussion and which for written work
■ ideas for support or extension work – including links to photocopiable worksheets, suggested resource books, etc.

For convenience, these detailed notes are gathered under the subheadings which are used in the Pupils' Book, e.g. *The Blitz begins* and *Morale* (pages 164–167). So if you are looking for notes in a hurry, the important information you need is the page number in the Pupils' Book and the subheading under which the item appears.

For each unit, there are also a number of photocopiable worksheets. These provide support and extension material. Some of them are designed to be suitable for homework where it is impossible for pupils to use the Pupils' Book.

## Using the material in the classroom

Before starting out on an enquiry always read the questions and activities in the Pupils' Book and the descriptions and suggestions in this Teachers' Book. Make sure the pupils know the aims of the enquiry or of any piece of work they are undertaking.

There are hundreds of questions in the book. Needless to say, they are not all intended for written work. The questions in the yellow boxes are often best used for class discussion. They are there to help pupils interrogate sources and to approach very gradually the issue which is posed in the enquiry. They are like stepping stones towards the summary question at the end of the enquiry. So all the questions should be addressed in class or group discussion in some way because they are designed either to introduce or to reinforce new ideas, skills and concepts. It may well be that pupils are asked to give a written response to only one question in four. We have made it clear in the detailed notes that follow when an exercise is particularly appropriate for oral work. Other questions require pupils to role-play, match, prioritise, etc. A wide range of learning techniques is used throughout.

Where a written response is suggested, there are occasions during the year when pupils should be actively encouraged to use word processors to produce their answers. It is an essential part of historical enquiry and communication to be able to present written conclusions clearly and neatly, to redraft conclusions in the light of new evidence, and to introduce new findings or further corroborating evidence into a written answer. Word processing facilities make this more feasible than before. So on occasions where an enquiry involves a wide range of source material or involves an element of presentation to the rest of the class, encourage pupils to use word processors. If you have DTP software available it will be very useful for activities such as those on pages 19 and 35 of the Pupils' Book. Other IT applications of History – e.g. databases to handle statistical data, graphics, concept keyboard, timeline software programmes, or historical simulations – can be introduced into the course easily at the teacher's discretion, where they will help serve the overall aim of making History enjoyable and accessible for all pupils.

A lot of tasks require group work, and many suggest the use of display or presentations. All these have implications for how you organise your classroom.

Sources are an integral part of the book – many spreads consist of almost nothing but sources. They are designed to be used; many of the questions within an enquiry are designed to ensure that pupils read, study and understand the source material provided, acquiring source-evaluation skills in the process.

Consistent with our aim of providing useful learning experiences for the pupils, we have translated, simplified and edited written source material to make it accessible. Make it clear to pupils that spelling and punctuation have been made contemporary. Modern equivalent words have been substituted where necessary, or definitions provided. Major edits have usually been shown by ellipses. However, the sense and meaning of all sources have been preserved.

The source line – which introduces and describes the source being studied – is an important tool for the pupil. It contains the details that pupils will need to know to answer any questions, such as who made or wrote the source and when. Encourage pupils to see these source lines as an important part of the evidence.

In the Pupils' Book we have deliberately kept the source line short, including only the information which we expect the student to need. Further information about some of the sources and some of the writers or artists has been provided in the detailed notes on each unit where it is helpful.

In most questions the reasons pupils give for their answers are as important as the answers themselves. In explaining why they have answered in a certain way they will reveal how deeply they have understood an issue. We have not, however, constantly reiterated in the questions 'explain your answer', as it gets highly repetitive. Pupils in Y9 should be aware that all historical answers require backing up by evidence. However, you might want to remind pupils of this more often than we have done.

## Differentiation

First-hand classroom experience of teaching from SHP's *Discovering the Past* series has made it clear that pupils of all abilities can tackle the type of questions and issues in this book, *provided that they are not overwhelmed by being given too many sources, and that the sources they do use are of a suitable level of difficulty.*

One successful approach with mixed ability classes is to have all pupils attempting the same tasks but to reduce the amount of source material for some of them. This can be done in a number of ways. Look, for example, at question 2 on page 133 – arguments for and against Appeasement. There are nine sources for pupils to consider. This might be far too much for some pupils. Therefore we suggest the following strategies:
■ You can divide the class into groups and ask each group to consider just one or two sources. The groups' findings can then be pooled.
■ Some groups can use just one source and others can use all the sources. This can be quite successfully done if the groups are carefully selected.
■ Instead of splitting the class into groups you can, with careful class management, give individual pupils different amounts of source material to use.

Another example might be in question 1 on page 21. Individual pupils can be given just one or two sources to use, and it is then the class as a whole which draws up the list of words to describe Arkwright's character.

As a general principle, as soon as it becomes clear that a pupil is finding a task difficult, the amount of material he/she is asked to use can be reduced. The important principle remains, however, that all pupils are

being posed the same questions, even if the amount of source material they are using is varied.

Strategies such as these should ensure that all pupils end up succeeding (at their own level) with each of the tasks in the book.

It is also important that pupils are not left alone to tackle each enquiry. The book has been written with the expectation that much of the material in the authors' text will be introduced by the teacher. It might be that the teacher reads a spread through beforehand and then uses the information it provides to set the scene for pupils before they proceed to the sources and questions.

It is also sound practice to read and discuss all sources with pupils. We are attempting to develop pupils' skills and understanding, which will not be achieved by simply leaving them to get on with the questions by themselves all the time.

Group work can also help here. Some pupils will contribute to small group discussion, and risk putting forward ideas and answers, in a way which they would not do in front of the whole class. We have all seen how pupils tend to experiment more in small groups, partly because they are not so worried about getting things wrong.

In this book pupils are working with new ideas, skills and problems for much of the time and we should not be surprised if their early attempts to answer a question fall well below what might be regarded as a good answer. However, any genuine attempts to tackle the questions should be encouraged – the teacher can then begin to suggest how such answers could be built on. If pupils are worried about 'getting it wrong' they will play safe and their progress will be hindered.

We have taken the needs of mixed ability teaching into consideration in designing the worksheets. For example, we have provided differentiated tasks on Worksheets 35 and 36, *Causes of the Second World War* and a differentiated sequencing exercise on Worksheet 45, *The war in Europe*.

The principle remains, however, that the overall historical question being posed remains the same for all abilities. What varies, and what determines the question's accessibility, is the amount of material pupils need to manipulate or take account of in answering that question.

Special Needs Support Materials, for teaching those with learning difficulties, is in preparation for both units (see page 126). The materials for each unit consist of a Picture Pack (reproducing 16 or more key visuals from the unit), teachers' notes and a pupil workbook for pupils using the Picture Pack; plus an extensive Teachers' Resource Book which includes a comprehensive range of photocopiable worksheets at different levels to improve access to both units for slower learners.

## Local history

If you have access to local resources relating to either of the units in this book you can design your own local history project. A sense of local chronology – of change over time in a local area – can help motivate pupils towards a broader interest in History and make them feel more fully a part of their local community.

The detailed notes for this book include a number of suggestions for local study. For example, the impact of the Industrial Revolution on your local area would be an obvious choice for schools in Britain's industrial heartland. Life on the Home Front during the Second World War would be a useful choice in almost all areas, and could successfully build on pupils' local history work in Key Stage 2.

### The Changing Role of Women

This supplementary unit focuses on British history – reviewing the periods studied in the British core units – and examines how and why the role of women changed during these periods.

It is long-term development study, which has its beginnings in pre-Norman Britain, yet takes pupils into the changes that occurred during the nineteenth century and into the twentieth century. It therefore sets pupils up with a useful perspective on Key Stage 3 as a whole. The individual enquiries are matched to particular units, so can be incorporated into your study of Britain 1750–1900. Additionally, as a compact and manageable development study, it paves the way for the more complex development studies which pupils may be studying for GCSE.

## LINKS AND CONNECTIONS ACROSS KEY STAGE 3

The *Discovering the Past* series has been designed from the beginning to encourage teachers to see the three-year course as a whole and to work with pupils on the links between units. Thus *Contrasts and Connections* (Y7) looked at links, contrasts and similarities between the Roman Empire, medieval British society and the Islamic Empire. In *Societies in Change* (Y8), the causes, nature and consequences of revolutions against the monarch in Britain and France are compared with each other. In this book, Britain 1750–1900 has been linked with The Twentieth-Century World through sections on the First World War.

Investigation of links between units will considerably enrich teaching and learning throughout the Key Stage 3 course. Thus, when pupils are studying society in The Making of the UK, constant reference should be made to similarities to and differences from society in the Middle Ages. This need not always involve written work, but such work should be attempted on occasions. The series includes opportunities for such work, for example, on page 26 of *Societies in Change*.

Here are two possibilities for an overall strategy to organise cross-unit work.

■ Historical perspectives could be used. These involve studying History from political, economic, technological and scientific, social, religious, and cultural and aesthetic perspectives. It would be possible, therefore, to devise a

'social' cross-unit theme from existing schemes of work. One approach might be to extract the 'social' elements of the Programmes of Study for the statutory units (remember that non-statutory units 5 and 6 could be used as well). For example:

| Unit | 'Social' content from Programme of Study |
| --- | --- |
| Roman Empire | ways of life in Rome and the provinces; family and society |
| Medieval Realms | feudalism and the structure of medieval society; health and disease, including the Black Death and its impact |
| The Making of the UK | social class in early modern Britain; regional differences in wealth and lifestyle |
| The French Revolution | living conditions of each of the estates before and after the revolution |
| Britain 1750–1900 | the impact of economic change on families and communities, working and living conditions, and the size and distribution of Britain's population; the impact of the Empire on the way of life of the British people |
| The Twentieth-Century World | the experience of war; the Holocaust; the Home Front in Britain; refugees. |

It is thus possible to identify some themes which range across the core units, e.g. working and living conditions, the family, and how these differed between social classes.

Large timelines could be used effectively to support such thematic work. Different groups within a class could be asked to compare societies using different criteria.

It is not suggested that we teach all the content through such themes, but that they are identified and returned to at regular intervals to provide opportunities for pupils to see links, similarities and contrasts between different societies and different times. It is also important to ensure that such work does not become merely descriptive. It should be used to raise questions about change and continuity, cause and consequence, similarity and difference.

■ Another way of planning cross-unit work would be to concentrate on the historical concepts listed in the Key Elements. These concepts, such as Empire, or monarch, need to be constantly revisited to deepen pupils' understanding. Comparisons could be made, for example, between the different ways in which the Roman and British Empires were acquired, were controlled, and declined.

Using a combination of the two approaches above, here are some suggestions for cross-unit exercises that can be developed using the three Key Stage 3 core texts in the *Discovering the Past* series.

■ Compare life and work in a medieval village with life and work in a late nineteenth-century village (*Contrasts and Connections* Unit B Section 3/*Peace and War* Unit A Section 4). This could be developed as a local history study of a village or town through the ages.

■ Look at some examples of King and Parliament coming into conflict and discuss how similar/different the causes/consequences were (*Contrasts and Connections* Unit B Section 4/*Societies in Change* Unit A Section 4).

■ Compare means of transport from one period to another (*Contrasts and Connections* Unit B Section 3/*Peace and War* Unit A Section 3).

■ Discuss who was more powerful: King John, King Charles I, or Queen Victoria (*Contrasts and Connections* Unit B Section 4/*Societies in Change* Unit A Section 4/*Peace and War* Unit A Section 6).

■ Compare the importance of religion in people's lives in the Middle Ages with its importance in the seventeenth and nineteenth centuries (*Contrasts and Connections* Unit B Section 3/*Societies in Change* Unit A Section 3/*Peace and War* Unit A Section 5).

■ Compare the role of Parliament in the thirteenth century with that in the nineteenth century (*Contrasts and Connections* Unit B Section 4/*Peace and War* Unit A Section 6).

■ Compare how war affected people's lives at different times in the past (*Contrasts and Connections* Unit B Section 2/*Societies in Change* Unit A Section 4 and Unit B Sections 3 and 4/*Peace and War* Unit B Section 3).

■ Compare why and how ordinary people protested in different times in the past (*Contrasts and Connections* Unit A Section 4 and Unit B Section 4/*Societies in Change* Unit A Section 4 and Unit B Sections 2 and 3/*Peace and War* Unit A Section 6).

## CROSS-CURRICULAR LINKS

Although cross-curricular themes are no longer specified in the National Curriculum, the need to develop cross-curricular links has not disappeared as part of good practice in teaching. This book will make a very useful contribution to cross-curricular learning. We have mentioned just a few examples below to illustrate the possibilities. Others are discussed in the detailed notes.

### Themes

In Britain 1750–1900 we are investigating a period when many features of British democracy were tested and reformed in the face of intense popular pressure. This gives plentiful opportunities, therefore, for developing education for Citizenship, and indeed this topic is tackled directly on pages 82–83, with a comparison of Britain's earlier political systems with our own system today.

In The Twentieth-Century World the key ideas of dictatorship and democracy are investigated in detail, and many parallels can be drawn with modern events.

Other, broader Citizenship questions are raised in Britain 1750–1900: assumptions about society and about the need to care for individuals are tackled in *Victorian values*; racism is approached directly by a number of enquiries (pages 70–75, for example); equality of work opportunities is investigated in *The Victorians and women workers* (pages 80–81); and the whole question of how people bring about change – what methods and what aims are appropriate – is the focus of pages 100–101, *Popular protest movements*.

In The Twentieth-Century World the question of war

crimes – who should be charged, how they should be tried, and how they should be punished – is a potent one for Citizenship education. It is raised at a number of points, not only in connection with the Holocaust, but also in connection with the Battle of the Atlantic, the bombing of Dresden and the atomic bombing of Japan.

Finally, both units give opportunity for furthering pupils' Economic and Industrial Understanding. Section 2 of Britain 1750–1900, *What made British business tick?*, consists of case studies of British entrepreneurs and rests on an analysis of the factors that make businesses grow.

In The Twentieth-Century World enquiries such as *The rise of the dictators* look at the impact of world recession on individual countries. Pupils' awareness of the links between economic problems and social fragmentation can be developed.

### Other subjects

Finally there are many links into other core and foundation subjects, and into RE. For example:

■ Science and Technology: the importance of scientific and technological skills in the emergence of industrial entrepreneurs such as Wedgwood or Arkwright, or in the contributions of inventors and technicians to the transport revolution, is explored in some detail.

■ Geography: the book provides a valuable historical perspective on geographical themes, such as urbanisation and the growth and development of settlements (in case studies of London, Brighton and Merthyr Tydfil), and of transport networks and the location of industry (particularly in the study of the Liverpool–Manchester area on pages 34–39).

Britain 1750–1900 also builds a framework for understanding the pattern of Britain's trade with the rest of the world. It highlights the strategic importance of ports such as Liverpool and London in that pattern of trade.

There is much map work, including at the largest scale early Ordnance Survey sheets (Worksheet 16), and at the smallest scale global maps (such as page 42), which show patterns and places in overview and help pupils build up their 'map of the world' alongside their 'map of the past'.

■ English: we have provided below a reading list of historical fiction which illuminates events or themes covered in the two units. These may be available through English departments or libraries, and can be used as part of pupils' work with English literature as well as for their historical value.

### Britain 1750–1900

*The Children of the House* by Philippa Pearce and Brian Fairfax-Lucy (changing life in a large country estate throughout the nineteenth century) (Puffin)
*Early Rising* by Joan Clarke (nineteenth century) (Cape)
*Smith* by Leon Garfield (eighteenth century) (Puffin)
*Black Jack* by Leon Garfield (adventure story set in mid-eighteenth-century London) (Puffin) and other books by Leon Garfield

*The Bonnie Pit Laddie* by Frederick Grice (a boy's fight to get out of the Durham pits in the early twentieth century) (Puffin)

*Midnight is a Place* by Joan Aiken (children working in a textile mill) (Puffin)

*Lark Rise to Candleford* by Flora Thomson (an isolated rural community in the 1880s) (Penguin)

*The Water Babies* by Charles Kingsley (a classic story of a chimneysweep's adventures) (Penguin)

books by Charles Dickens, e.g. *Oliver Twist*, *Great Expectations* (difficult for independent reading for this age group)

## The Twentieth-Century World

*Fireweed* by Jill Paton Walsh (runaway children during the Blitz) (Puffin)

*The Dolphin Crossing* by Jill Paton Walsh (Dunkirk) (Macmillan)

*The House of Sixty Fathers* by Meindert De Jong (war between China and Japan) (Puffin)

*I am David* by Anne Holm (refugees) (Puffin)

*We Couldn't Leave Dinah* by Mary Threadgold (the Channel Islands under German occupation) (Puffin)

*The Captive Isle* by Veronica Robinson (the Channel Islands) (Dent)

*The House on the Common* by Alison Prince (life during the War) (Methuen)

*In Spite of all the Terror* by Hester Burton (from evacuation to post-war problems) (OUP)

*Dangerous Spring/The Ark* both by Margot Benary (the end of the War and life after for a German family) (Macmillan)

*War Boy* by Michael Foreman (childhood in the country) (Pavilion)

*Dawn of Fear* by Susan Cooper (the Blitz) (Puffin)

*When Hitler Stole Pink Rabbit* by Judith Kerr (Jewish family's escape from Nazi Germany) (Armada)

*Friedrich/I Was There* both by Hans Peter Richter (pre-war Nazi Germany) (Puffin)

*The Silver Sword* by Ian Serrailler (refugees) (Puffin)

*Goodnight, Mister Tom* by Michelle Magorian (evacuation) (Puffin)

*Carrie's War* by Nina Bawden (evacuation) (Puffin)

*The Machine Gunners/Fathom Five* both by Robert Westall (the Blitz) (Puffin)

*The Diary of Anne Frank* (Pan)

*Fight for the Sky* by Douglas Bader (Fontana)

*Fly West* by Ivan Southall (flying boats) (Puffin)

## Television programmes

*History in Action* series (ITV):
    The Siege of Leningrad
    The League of Nations
    Il Duce
    Tiger at the Gate (the rise of Hitler)
    The Master Race
*History File* series (BBC):
    Why Appeasement?
    Hitler's Germany

Stalin and the Modernisation of Russia
Make Germany Pay (Versailles)

## ASSESSMENT

### How do we deal with the Attainment Target?

In the revised National Curriculum a single attainment target for History has replaced the original three. This has been done to:
■ emphasise the interrelatedness of the various elements of knowledge, understanding and skills
■ avoid fragmentation and an artificial divide between content and skills.

The enquiries and questions in *Peace and War* have been devised to reinforce this approach. The book is divided into a number of major enquiries. Pupils are encouraged to use their knowledge, skills and understanding to come to their own conclusions on the various issues. As we have explained on p.10, the major exercises in the blue boxes are designed to allow pupils to do this. They involve pupils bringing together these various elements to produce descriptions, narratives, analyses and explanations of the past. They are thus able to plan and produce substantial pieces of work.

However, pupils need first to be taken through the material step by step. This is the function of the yellow box exercises. These often have narrower targets, e.g. to highlight causation. They do not all have to be attempted through written work. Some can be used for class discusssion, others can be ignored. It is up to you to decide what is most appropriate for your pupils.

The level descriptions of the Attainment Target cover the following aspects of pupils' performance:
■ their **chronological** understanding
■ the **range and depth** of their historical knowledge and understanding
■ their ability to use their historical knowledge and understanding to **analyse interpretations** of history
■ their ability to use their knowledge and understanding of history to **analyse sources** of historical information
■ their ability to **communicate** their historical knowledge and understanding.

These are the areas in which pupils should be given opportunities to make progress.

However, it is important to remember that the level descriptions should be used in their entirety for summative assessment. They are not to be used:
■ for marking single pieces of work
■ for formative assessment
■ as targets for questions or tasks
■ as learning or teaching objectives
■ as a list of things to be assessed.

You should not attempt to take the pupils through the levels. This will lead to artificial and sterile work being done. The tasks in the book have not been designed for that purpose.

For planning purposes therefore, it is important to use the Key Elements. If coverage of these is built into teaching and learning programmes, the requirements of the level descriptions will be met.

The new order has been structured so that these five axes of progression within the level descriptions are also the five areas of the Key Elements.

| Aspects of the level descriptions | Key Elements |
| --- | --- |
| **Chronological** understanding | 1. Chronology |
| **Range and depth** of historical knowledge and understanding | 2. Range and depth of historical knowledge and understanding |
| Ability to use historical knowledge and understanding to **analyse interpretations** of history | 3. Interpretations of history |
| Ability to use knowledge and understanding of history to **analyse sources** of historical information | 4. Historical enquiry |
| Ability to **communicate** historical knowledge and understanding | 5. Organisation and communication |

All of the Key Elements have been covered in this book - this means that the Attainment Target and the level descriptions have also been covered.

## KEY ELEMENTS

The Key Elements are closely related and should be developed through the Study Units, as appropriate. Not all the Key Elements need to be developed in each Study Unit.

Pupils should be taught:

■ **1. Chronology**

**a** to place the events, people and changes in the periods studied within a chronological framework;

**b** to use dates, terms and conventions that describe historical periods and the passing of time, e.g. *era, medieval, Reformation, Industrial Revolution, Hanoverian, Georgian.*

■ **2. Range and depth of historical knowledge and understanding**

**a** to analyse the characteristic features of particular periods and societies, including the range of ideas, beliefs and attitudes of people, and the experiences of men and women; and to analyse the social, cultural, religious and ethnic diversity of the societies studied;

**b** to describe, analyse and explain reasons for and results of the historical events, situations and changes in the periods studied;

**c** to develop overviews of the main events and changes, both within and across periods, by making links between the content in different study units and between local, British, European and world history;

**d** to assess the significance of the main events, people and changes studied.

■ **3. Interpretations of history**

**a** how and why some historical events, people, situations and changes have been interpreted differently;

**b** to analyse and evaluate interpretations.

■ **4. Historical enquiry**

**a** to investigate independently aspects of the periods studied, using a range of sources of information, including documents and printed sources, artefacts, pictures, photographs and films, music and oral accounts, buildings and sites;

**b** to ask and answer significant questions, to evaluate sources in their historical context, identify sources for an investigation, collect and record information relevant to a topic and reach conclusions.

■ **5. Organisation and communication**

**a** to recall, select and organise historical information, including dates and terms;

**b** to organise their knowledge and understanding of history through the accurate selection and deployment of terms necessary to describe and explain the periods and topics studied, including government, Parliament, Church, state, Empire, monarchy, republic, treaty, revolution, reform, class, nobility, peasantry, law, trade, industrialisation, Communism, Fascism, democracy, dictatorship;

**c** to communicate their knowledge and understanding of history, using a range of techniques, including extended narratives and descriptions, and substantiated explanations.

## How do we deal with the Key Elements?

### 1. Chronology

(a) Pupils' chronological understanding is developed in a number of ways.

Firstly, there are overall timelines of the major events for each of the two units on pages i–1 and 108–109.

In Britain 1750–1900 a chronological approach is not always appropriate, but regular overviews have been used to give pupils clear chronological summaries, e.g. *Popular protest movements* on pages 100–101.

The organisation of The Twentieth-Century World, on the other hand, is strictly chronological, giving pupils a clear view of how events unfolded.

Additionally, in The Twentieth-Century World, timelines are provided to give pupils an overview of both the main events leading up to the Second World War (pages 127–131) and the events of the War itself (pages 150–151).

Finally, *Peace and War* also includes several exercises requiring pupils to construct timelines themselves.

Teachers can supplement all these approaches to chronology by building up a class timeline of the main events of a unit as they are covered. This could be displayed on the classroom wall and could include pupils' work.

(b) The terminology historians use to organise events in the past such as era, Industrial Revolution, Victorian, and century has been used extensively throughout both units.

### 2. Range and depth of historical knowledge and understanding

(a) The characteristic features of societies during each period have been investigated in different ways – through contrasting case studies such as those of Ashill (pages 26–29 and 52–55) or Merthyr Tydfil (pages 56–59); or through more generalised case studies such as *What was life like in Nazi Germany?* (pages 122–123).

The diversity of society in these periods has also been covered, although there are obviously more opportunities to meet this requirement in Britain 1750–1900 than in The Twentieth-Century World. The social diversity of British society during the period 1750–1900 is considered by looking at how different social classes were affected by change in both town and village. Case studies are drawn from around Wales, Scotland and England. The values of different classes are studied, as are their varying attitudes towards reform of different types. Cultural diversity is shown in the enquiries on Brighton and on Victorian values, while the latter also investigates religious diversity (with additional extension material provided on Worksheet 18). Finally, case studies of Sake Deen Mahomed and of black people in Britain encourage an awareness of Britain's ethnic diversity.

In The Twentieth-Century World social diversity is also studied through a consideration of how people from different classes experienced evacuation.

The experiences of men and women have not been ignored. They are integrated into the main coverage of both units in a natural way, but there are also some places where they provide the main focus; examples are *The story of two families* (pages 50–51), Section 5 *Victorian values* (pages 64–81), and the enquiry into the match workers' strike (pages 98–99) in Britain 1750–1900, and the study of the role of women during the War on pages 168–169 of The Twentieth-Century World.

(b) One of the main features of the book is the opportunity it gives pupils to describe, analyse and explain the reasons for and the results of the main events, developments and changes. Such opportunities are provided for the development of British industry (pages 8–23) or the outbreak of the Second World War (pages 118–149), for example.

(c) Pupils are given numerous opportunities to learn about aspects of each unit in depth and even through a local context. The book, organised as it is as a series of major enquiries, is really a series of studies in depth – as we have already explained on pages 6–9. Unit A also abounds with local case studies, such as those of Ashill, Merthyr Tydfil, Brighton and London, instead of presenting a stereotypical composite village, town or city.

Opportunities have also been created for pupils to develop clear overviews of the main events and changes across each unit, as we have explained on pages 6 and 8.

(d) This Key Element also requires pupils to assess the significance of the main events, personalities and developments. This matches one of the main aims of the book – to allow pupils to make their own judgements about developments such as the Industrial Revolution (*Was there an Industrial Revolution?*), personalities such as Hitler and Churchill, or events such as the dropping of the atomic bomb.

### 3. Interpretations of history

Several opportunities are created for pupils to consider how and why some events and personalities have been interpreted differently, e.g.Victorian values (pages 64–69) or the figures involved in the abolition of slavery (pages 82–84).In the enquiry *Hitler's War* (pages 124–131) pupils are presented with the conventional view that Hitler caused the Second World War, then subsequent enquiries (pages 132–149) focus on other causes, culminating in pupils comparing the views of A.J.P. Taylor and Alan Bullock on what caused the war.

### 4. Historical enquiry

(a) The book uses many different types of sources:

(i) **written sources:** government regulations, reports of government commissions, letters, diaries, tourist guides, directories, advertisements, political manifestos, pamphlets, autobiographies, parliamentary speeches, memoirs, newspapers, magazines, poems, institutional records (e.g. court and prison), exhibition guides, textbooks and academic books

(ii) **pictorial sources:** engravings, photographs, paintings, cartoons, drawings, posters, woodcuts

(iii) **other types of sources:** plans, maps, graphs, statistics, flow diagrams, artists' reconstructions.

While it is not possible to provide artefacts, buildings or oral evidence in a textbook, we have used photographs of plaques, beer mats, pottery and buildings, stills from films, and extracts from speeches or interviews.

The blue-boxed activities and summary questions allow students to use this wide range of source material to investigate major issues of the period.

**(b)** The book abounds with questions requiring students to use, interpret and evaluate source material. These range from tightly focused questions, perhaps just on a single source, to major pieces of work for which students have to select material across an entire enquiry.

### 5. Organisation and communication

**(a)** Almost every enquiry in the book provides exercises (in particular the activities and summary questions) where pupils are encouraged to identify relevant sources for an investigation, organise their material, and then present their conclusions in a variety of ways.

The questions in yellow boxes are more limited in scope and act as valuable steps along the way to the major piece of work at the end of each enquiry.

For some of the major activities and questions, worksheets are provided in this Teachers' Book which will help pupils to organise the large amount of material they are being asked to work with.

**(b)** The book gives plentiful opportunities for pupils to learn to use key historical terms. In fact coverage of some of these key terms has been one of the planning principles of *Peace and War*. The table below shows which key terms and concepts are covered where.

| Term/concept | Britain 1750–1900 | The Twentieth-Century World |
|---|---|---|
| government | 86–95 | |
| Parliament | 86–95 | |
| state | 64–67, 76–79 | 118 |
| Empire | 42–45, 70–75 | |
| treaty | | 116–117, 136–137, 138–139 |
| revolution | 48–49, 88–90 | |
| reform | 82–101 | |
| class | 82–101 | 154–157 |
| trade | 32–45, 68–69 | |
| industrialisation | 8–25, 48–49, 56–59 | |
| Communism | | 118–119, 208–210 |
| Fascism | | 119–125, 186–193 |
| democracy | 86–87 | 118, 208–210 |
| dictatorship | | 118–123 |

Of course, pupils should have been introduced to some of these concepts in Y7 or Y8. On pages 12–13 we outlined methods by which these concepts could be used for developing links and connections between units.

Other concepts, such as Fascism and Communism, will be encountered for the first time in Y9. This has been borne in mind, and you will see that concepts such as Communism, Fascism, dictatorship and democracy are given clear and careful introductions (pages 86–87, 118–122).

**(c)** Pupils are asked to use a wide range of techniques to communicate their conclusions, including essays, posters, group presentations, dramatic reconstructions, etc.

### A variety of perspective

There is one other feature of the book which is just as important as the Key Elements: its coverage of history from a variety of perspectives, economic, social, cultural and political. Below are some examples from each unit of opportunities for pupils to study history from a range of perspectives. It should be remembered that although the areas below identify the main perspective used in various enquiries, this does not mean that other perspectives are not present. Many of the enquiries are approached from a range of perspectives.

| Perspective | Example |
|---|---|
| political | *How did people bring about change?* *The causes of the Second World War* *The role of wartime leaders* *A better world* |
| economic, technological, scientific | *What made British business tick?* *What caused the Industrial Revolution?* |
| social | *Was life getting better?* *Victorian values* *What was life like during the War?* |
| religious | *Victorian values* |
| cultural and aesthetic | *Victorian values* *The two faces of London* |

### Formative assessment

If the level descriptions are not to be used to mark pieces of work or to measure the progress of pupils month by month, how is formative assessment to be carried out?

It is spurious to suggest that pupils' progress in History can be measured exactly. But it is possible to identify weaknesses and strengths to help them make progress. Do not attempt to measure pupils' work against the level descriptions. Rather, look at their work and ask yourself the questions 'How good an answer is this to the question/task I set?' and 'What are the strengths and weaknesses of this answer?'. This is a more meaningful approach than to ask yourself 'Does this piece of work display level 4 understanding of causation?'.

Of course, you will end up identifying weaknesses and strengths which are related to particular areas of understanding and skills such as causation or evaluating sources, but it is better to measure these against what you would consider a good answer to the question you set than against some external criteria such as level descriptions. To help you in this process we have included advice in the detailed notes on which areas particular questions or activities are targeting. For example, if the question asked was 'What does this picture tell you about the people it shows?' there is little point in marking a pupil's work level 1. What would be useful would be a comment such as 'A good detailed description of what the people in the picture are wearing. Can you try to use this to work out whether they were rich or poor?'

**PEACE & WAR**

Remember that many of the exercises deliberately involve pupils using a range of knowledge, skills and understanding; so while in assessing a pupil's work you may not find much evidence of the skills you or we originally targeted, you may find valuable evidence of other qualities. Remember to keep in mind the question we suggested above: 'How good an answer is this to the question I set?'.

For formative assessment it is useful to have some indication of what constitutes progress. This is an area fraught with difficulties and the following is presented more as a practical working aid than as the definitive statement on the subject.

Despite the demise of the three Attainment Targets, the five areas of understanding and skill in them still underpin National Curriculum History and can still be used for formative assessment:
- historical change and continuity
- historical cause and consequence
- key features of societies and periods
- interpretations of history
- the use of historical sources.
  We can add to these
- the ability to carry out an enquiry and communicate conclusions.

In each of these we can identify clear stages of development:

## Historical change and continuity
**Stage i** an awareness of time and sequence, and an ability to use common terms, and to sequence things and events
**Stage ii** an ability to recognise and describe change – its nature and its pace
**Stage iii** an ability to analyse, evaluate and make judgements about the pace, nature and impact of change

## Historical cause and consequence
**Stage i** an awareness that things happen for a reason – usually pupils at this stage think things happen simply because people make them happen
**Stage ii** an understanding that events have causes and consequences, and that these can be impersonal and can be grouped together
**Stage iii** an ability to analyse, evaluate and make judgements about causes and consequences

## Key features of societies and periods
**Stage i** an awareness of differences between the present and times in the past
**Stage ii** knowledge and understanding of distinctive features of times in the past
**Stage iii** knowledge and understanding of the variety of ideas and attitudes in past times

## Interpretations of history
**Stage i** an awareness of the different ways in which the past is represented
**Stage ii** an understanding of how different interpretations  come about

**Stage iii** an ability to analyse and evaluate different interpretations

## The use of historical sources
**Stage i**  an ability to extract or infer information
**Stage ii** an ability to use sources critically
**Stage iii** an ability to analyse sources in context

## The ability to carry out an enquiry and communicate conclusions
**Stage i** a readiness to pose and answer their own questions about the past from material provided by the teacher
**Stage ii** an ability to identify and collect sources suitable for an enquiry and to communicate their conclusions
**Stage iii** an ability to structure their enquiries and communication independently

These stages are not substitutes for the level descriptions and pupils should not be moved through them in order. Each stage needs constant revisiting. However, one would expect pupils to be able to operate within each of these areas of skill and understanding in increasingly sophisticated ways. This can be encouraged by gradually making more demands in the following areas:
- the amount of source material and the number of different sources used
- the complexity and length of the source material used
- the level of complexity at which the events are studied
- how familiar pupils already are with the content
- how far the content is structured for easier assimilation
- how far the task has been structured
- how complex the task is
- how much support is provided by the teacher
- whether pupils work individually or in groups
- whether they respond orally, visually, or in writing.
  It is also important to look for the following qualities in pupils' answers:
- the breadth and depth of knowledge used
- historical accuracy
- selection and relevance of information
- planning and organisation
- independence, initiative and imagination, ability to make links, comparisons and contrasts
- critical analysis
- quality of explanations
- effective communication
- balance
- ability to generalise.

## Summative assessment
When you have to summarise and report on pupils' progress at the end of a year or the end of a Key Stage, you will then have to use the eight-level scale - for the first time. Each level description provides an overview of the key features of typical performance at that level. You will not find any pupils whose performance matches

any one level description exactly. Rather than expecting
to do this, you should identify the level which fits the
pupil better than other levels do. You will find yourself
thinking that a particular pupil appears to show some of
the qualities described in e.g. levels 3, 4 and 5. Go for
the level description which is the best fit rather than
hoping for an exact fit.

Remember that you are summarising the pupils'
attainment. So you need to base your judgement on an
overall view of the pupil. You will need to review their
attainment across a period of time and across several
pieces of work. This may involve collecting a portfolio of
work from each pupil on a regular basis, or simply
glancing through their exercise book and your mark
book. You also need to take into account what you know
about the pupil as the person who has been teaching
them History for a year or more. How well do they
perform in group work, in class discussions, and so on?
Can they produce work of a certain quality only when
you give them a lot of help and support?

# BRITAIN 1750–1900

# *Introduction*

**Britain 1750–1900** is a core unit in the National Curriculum. On pages 4–18 we explain how best to meet the requirements of the revised curriculum in your teaching of this unit.

The unit begins with three snapshots of Britain in 1750, 1825 and 1900 to give pupils an overview of some of the changes that are going to be investigated.

In Sections 2 and 3 the focus is on the Industrial Revolution, Section 2 looking mainly at the entrepreneurs and Section 3 at other causes of the Industrial Revolution.

The remainder of the unit looks in some detail at the impact of these changes on ordinary people. Section 4 does so through a series of four case studies of people and places, Section 5 through an investigation of Victorian values and Section 6 through an investigation of various popular protest movements.

## AIMS OF THE UNIT

■ The unit covers a period of rapid and intense change in many areas of British society. New industries were developing, new jobs were created. New methods of transport were introduced, and new techniques in farming were adopted. Towns were growing, villages were declining. Population was growing, but in the towns public health problems were also growing.

One of the primary aims of this unit is therefore to investigate these changes, the reasons for them and their consequences for individuals.

Pupils will begin to see some of the complexities of analysing change. They will see that change takes place at different rates at different times and in different places. They will be introduced to the idea that in some areas of British industry very little changed between 1750 and 1900.

■ The second major aim of this unit is to investigate causation or to look at reasons for and results of events.

Pupils will be introduced to a range of individual causal factors and will see how each one contributed to the Industrial Revolution, before being introduced to the essentially complex relationship between these factors and to the arguments for and against each one as the primary cause.

Later in the unit there are many individual case studies, e.g. those into factory reform, the abolition of slavery, or the 1832 Reform Act, which also investigate a range of issues to do with causation.

■ Throughout the unit there is an attempt to see society in the round. Increasingly pupils will be able to see that life for residents of an industrial town such as Merthyr Tydfil was not necessarily the same as for residents of a rural village or a London tenement.

■ The nineteenth century is a rich vein for looking at different interpretations of history. The Victorian age itself casts a long shadow over the twentieth century,

and opinions about the achievements and the failures of the Victorians differ widely even today.

We have consciously investigated this issue in Section 5 *Victorian values*, and in the final enquiry, *Images of the Victorians*.

■ Source-based enquiry is the mainstay of the unit, as it is of the entire series. Visual sources and written sources are presented as part of every spread, and using them is essential for all the pupil tasks.

We aim to provide as much original source material as possible for pupils to work with, including government reports, autobiography, letters, paintings, cartoons, handbills and posters – you will even find a biscuit tin, a video jacket and Christmas cards.

## FURTHER READING

You will find it useful to consult in more detail many of the modern historical works from which the written sources have been taken. These are each described in the source lines throughout the unit.

Additionally, we would recommend Asa Briggs' *From Iron Bridge to Crystal Palace* as an excellent survey of the period.

Many of the primary written sources from this period, e.g. Robert Owen's works quoted on pages 20–21, are also available through libraries.

Historical fiction related to the period is listed on pages 13–14.

# Detailed notes

## Section 1: Introduction

### ENQUIRY: BRITAIN 1750–1900: WHAT CHANGED?

Pupils' Book pp. 2–7
Worksheet 1

This is an introductory enquiry, which aims to provide pupils with a framework or mental map of the unit as a whole. The three spreads give snapshots of 1750, 1825 and 1900, with the information grouped clearly into several categories or topics:

- Population
- Work
- Health and medicine
- Transport
- Culture
- Politics.

These topics reflect the broad concerns of the unit as a whole.

However, it is important to recognise from the outset that these categories are not sacrosanct. There are many links and overlaps between categories, for example between Population and Health and medicine. It can indeed be a fruitful exercise to ask pupils to identify overlaps or possible links between the various categories.

This enquiry can be used in several different ways:
*(i)* The first spread can be used as a link between The Making of the UK and Britain 1750–1900. In particular, if *Societies in Change* (the Y8 book in this series) has been used, pupils can recap their work on pages 88–93 (Defoe's tour of Britain) as a background for this first spread in Britain 1750–1900. *Societies in Change* gives a much broader picture of Britain as a whole in 1750 than is possible here, so pupils will be able to investigate each category on pages 2–3 in much greater depth.
*(ii)* The three spreads, including the questions, can provide an overview of broad patterns of change over the period 1750–1900. The questions focus mainly on change over the period.

There is a progression in the questions. Those on the first spread (pages 2–3) are limited to the sources on that spread. They aim to compare pupils' lives today with life in 1750, while involving a great deal of interrogation of the sources. The questions on the second spread (pages 4–5) pick up more complex ideas and progress from simple identification of changes between 1750 and 1825 to a consideration of different rates of change and responses to and consequences of change. The third spread (pages 6–7) continues the progression. It goes beyond simple descriptions of change: questions 5, 6 and 7 invite an analysis of change.
*(iii)* Instead of using the questions provided in the Pupils' Book, you could divide the class into groups, with each group considering change in one topic or 'category'

across all three spreads. Pupils should still be encouraged to ask questions such as: 'How much change has there been?' or 'Has change been for the better?' Each group could report its findings back to the class.
*(iv)* You could use **Worksheet 1**, if you think your pupils can cope with it at this stage. It involves pupils finding their way around the rest of the unit and carrying out some research.

Alternatively, this worksheet can be used at the end of the unit, after the pupils have covered some of the topics in depth.

(Pages 2–3)

### Work

**Question 2** could be used for Source 3 as well as for Source 4.

### Culture

**Source 7:** We have made a special point in this unit of helping students to do detailed interrogation of nineteenth-century paintings such as this (see page 35 of these Teachers' Notes).

### Politics

There is a graph summarising the gradual extension of the franchise on page 39 of these notes.

**Question 1:** Draw up a grid for pupils to do this exercise. Alternatively, one wall of the classroom could have information about 1750, and another information relating to today.

The death rate today is just over eleven per 1000.

(Pages 4–5)

### Work

**Source 9:** All the towns marked had over 100,000 population – the different sized circles are an attempt to show, very approximately, the relative sizes of the cities.

**Source 10:** The winding machinery is driven by the large drive wheel at the top of the picture – which at this date would probably be driven by water power.

### Transport

**Source 13:** Point out to pupils the wide-wheeled wagon in the left foreground.

(Pages 6–7)

### Transport

**Source 20:** This was in fact drawn as a plan for the Embankment when work was undertaken in 1862. Note also the overground railway. The station is Charing Cross, the bridge Hungerford.

The numbering was on the original plan and has not been added by us. Label 4 indicates a projected pneumatic railway.

**Source 21** is a detail from Source 2 on page 106, a painting made to celebrate the achievements of the Victorian era.

**Summary question 1:** Pupils will need two separate vertical axes. Population should be presented as a block graph, death rate as a line graph superimposed upon it. This is a technique of data presentation that pupils should be familiar with from work in other subjects, such as Geography. You could use graphics software on a computer.

Suggest to the pupils a scale for each axis. Put population on the left-hand axis, with a scale of 2 cm per 10 million population. Put death rate on the right-hand axis, with a scale of 2 cm for ten deaths per thousand. This scale exaggerates the rates of change in each factor, which should help pupils to see the relationship between the two.

**Questions 2–7:** Note what we said at the beginning of this enquiry about alternative ways of using the material on these three spreads.

**Question 7:** Remind pupils to give their reasons, as always. We have not constantly reiterated this, because at this stage in their work pupils should be doing so as a matter of course. You might want to remind them of this more often than we have done.

Having completed this introductory overview, you might like to set the agenda for the rest of the unit in terms of an analysis of the changes they have observed.

■ We are going to be looking further into some of these changes, asking what changed, how it changed and whether they were changes for the better.

■ We will try to discover reasons for these changes, and the consequences of these changes.

■ We will see what it was like to live during this period, and how people reacted to the changes.

■ We will see how historians have interpreted and explained the changes and developments in many different ways.

Which area you choose to focus on will of course depend on which aspects of the unit you choose to study in depth.

Some schools have found it very successful at this stage (or instead of pages 2–7) to use the story of the families as an overview, to personalise the changes being discussed.

## Section 2: What made British business tick?

All too often the development of British industry during the eighteenth and nineteenth centuries is presented as a list of inventions. We have tried to challenge this emphasis throughout Section 2 by looking at the wide range of factors which made British business tick. We have tried to highlight the role played by individuals – to see them not just as inventors but as entrepreneurs who were responsible for using the inventions, investing

capital, finding new ways to organise workers and expanding their markets.

This section could develops pupils' Economic and Industrial Understanding.

The entire section, or any of the individuals it studies, could form the basis for your depth study.

### ENQUIRY: WHY DID BUSINESSES GROW?

Pupils' Book pp. 8–9
Worksheets 2, 3

In this single-spread enquiry we have attempted to summarise the main factors that help businesses to grow. Some of them are illustrated in the story of Wedgwood (Source 4).

The key element of this spread is, however, the list of factors. This will form the background for substantial pupil work over the next few enquiries. A number of support worksheets and other learning devices have been supplied to help pupils organise and understand the various factors (notably Worksheets 2, 3 and 7).

(Page 8)

**Sources 1–3:** You might substitute slides or photos of other industries and businesses to show a wider range of machinery and numbers of employees.

**Questions 1–3:** The same questions can be asked about businesses today, which still come in all shapes and sizes – from the corner shop to the major industrial plant of the multinational corporation.

**Activity:** This is an attempt to get pupils to use the list of factors. There is clear evidence in the picture strip that Josiah Wedgwood took his product to new places and advertised it (Factor 1), improved transport, plant and technology (Factor 2), and reinvested money in better facilities for workers and better buildings (Factor 3).

You can find out more about Wedgwood, if you'd like to develop pupils' work on him as a depth study, in Lorna Weatherill, *The Pottery Trade in North Staffordshire (1660–1760)*. Alternatively, if appropriate, you could substitute the story of a local business in your area which grew up in the eighteenth and nineteenth centuries.

**Worksheet 2** can be introduced at this stage as a way of structuring this activity. It can also be used alongside later enquiries and most notably for question 2 on page 25 (Boulton and Watt), at which point comparisons can be drawn between the various businessmen studied.

The worksheet can also serve as an aid to organising material for an essay on any of the businessmen studied in Section 2. Note that pupils have been given the option of writing about one businessman or several of them. You may want to advise some pupils on which option to take.

There are other strategies through which pupils can be introduced to this important list of factors in the growth of businesses. For example, you may wish to give pupils just the three headings, and then ask them in three groups or in a class discussion to suggest points that might come under each heading. If that is too daunting, you might write up the headings and some of the points on the board to begin a brainstorm and ask pupils to suggest other points under each heading. It is more than likely that pupils will come up with more factors than we have done!

**Worksheet 3** is a support worksheet on these factors. It does not include all the factors – the idea is to simplify. We have selected just six of the most concrete factors, in particular those that an entrepreneur had some control over. It is an alternative to Worksheet 2, and like the latter can be used at any point in the section or filled in as you go along.

(Page 9)

**Question 1:** You can bring some everyday Victorian objects into the classroom to get pupils started.

## ENQUIRY: THE DARBYS OF COALBROOKDALE

Pupils' Book pp. 10–11
Worksheet 2

This single-spread enquiry allows pupils to see how a single business enterprise grew over three generations. It also serves to lay the foundations for an understanding of the iron industry, which is an essential background to pages 56–59 later in the book.

We take a deliberately accelerated journey through the eighteenth century, and you might like to build the class's work around a timeline for 1700–1800, showing the development of the Darbys' businesses.

If you wish to concentrate on Coalbrookdale in more depth there is an excellent pack called *Time and Money*, produced jointly by BP Education Service and the Ironbridge Gorge Museum Trust. The pack includes source material and questions, teachers' notes, colour slides and a game entitled 'Entrepreneur'. The pack covers the expansion of the Darby business, the role of the workers and the running of the company. The slides are particularly useful for investigating the different ways in which Coalbrookdale was portrayed by artists, as is *A View from the Iron Bridge*, published by the Ironbridge Gorge Trust.

(With thanks to Terry Fiehn for ideas and material.)

### Why Coalbrookdale?

**Question 1:** Source 1 is a deliberately simplified map of the area to highlight the components needed for the iron works: wood for charcoal, coal for coke, iron ore, limestone, transport, water supply. Pupils might note also the importance of the iron-making tradition.

### Abraham Darby I

**Question 1** is ideal for class discussion. In this question, as in so many in this section, it is important to challenge the idea of a lonely inventor working away in a cellar. Many industrial developments are a product of the very ordinary everyday factors listed here.

### Abraham Darby II

**Question 1:** Source 3 is called *The Upper Works at Coalbrookdale*. Note: coking is taking place on the right-hand side, next to the Furnace Pool; steel tubing (for a steam engine?) is being transported by horse-drawn carriage along the Wellington Road to (or from) the Coalbrookdale works; the horse-powered tramway cannot be seen but went up the steep path on the far side; the blast furnaces are on the left in the middle foreground; the pond (fed by the River Severn, which is out of view) supplied the water to the water wheels; the road on the right was called Darby Road; the workers' cottages are on the opposite slopes.

**Question 2:** Pupils might note that the smoke seems to disappear in mid-air. A more realistic picture of industrial pollution in Coalbrookdale is shown in pictures such as *Morning View of Coalbrookdale* by William Williams (1777), which is reproduced in the two publications mentioned above.

### Abraham Darby III

**Source 4:** The date of the jug is late (1856), but representations of the iron bridge such as this were very common from the end of the eighteenth century onwards, actively encouraged by the Darby family, who saw the power of the bridge for advertising purposes.

**Activity:** Many of the factors mentioned on the previous spread can be reinforced here. A preparation for the activity would therefore be to use **Worksheet 2** again and ask pupils (in groups) to consider how many of the factors are relevant to the Coalbrookdale story.

An alternative preparatory stage is to compare the development of this business with that of Wedgwood. Are the same factors at work?

On a DTP system you could create a letterhead for each of the generations of the Darby family.

## ENQUIRY: WHAT MADE RICHARD ARKWRIGHT SUCCESSFUL?

Pupils' Book pp. 12–15
Worksheets 2, 4

In this two-spread enquiry we examine the story of Richard Arkwright. The initial focus is on establishing the chronology of the growth of his business. We then examine how he operated as a businessman and the nature of his mills, and the factors which made him successful. We also investigate perceptions of Arkwright and his mills from his lifetime to the present day.

(Pages 12–13)

### Richard Arkwright's story

**Question 1:** It is important that pupils have an idea of the chronology. Question 1 can be completed with the aid of **Worksheet 4**.

**Question 2:** We think the artist was standing on the road running alongside the River Derwent, in the centre of the map.

(Pages 13–15)

### What were Arkwright's mills like?

**Source 8:** Note that the main mill building has had its top storey removed.

**Question 2:** Alternatively, select three descriptions at random and ask the class to match these to one of Sources 5, 7 or 8.

### Why was Arkwright successful?

**Questions 1–4:** You might well want to go through Sources 9–16 carefully with the whole class before attempting these questions. There are some difficult ideas and words.

**Question 1:** You could give pupils a list of ten possible words to choose from.

**Question 3:** If you prefer to use this question for class discussion, read Sources 9–16 carefully together. Then draw up on the board at the front of the class a 'league table' of the sources according to how much they admire Arkwright, the most admiring at the top and the most critical at the bottom.

**Summary question 1:** If this appears too difficult for your class, allow pupils to form groups of eight. In each of these groups tell two pupils to gather the evidence for each heading. The group can then 'pool' its findings. Again, **Worksheet 2** can be used.

**Activity:** An extra dimension can be added to this by asking different pupils to write obituaries for different types of newspaper, e.g. a popular sensationalist paper, a serious paper, a paper produced by working-class radicals, a paper for business people. The distinctive styles of some of today's equivalent papers – *The Sun*, *The Guardian*, the *Daily Mirror*, the *Financial Times* – could be briefly examined first to prepare for the activity.

## ENQUIRY: CHILDREN IN THE MILLS

Pupils' Book pp. 16–19

This two-spread enquiry creates something of a change of pace. The pupils have had a lot of new information to tackle in the preceding case studies of entrepreneurs, and many will find this enquiry rather less demanding and therefore a welcome break. It contains much vivid material which many pupils will be able to relate to.

Although the enquiry starts by looking at the general question of where businesses got their workers from, it soon focuses on child labour. The stress is on conditions in the mills and attitudes towards child workers.

This enquiry is also important as preparation for the subsequent enquiry about Robert Owen.

(Pages 16–17)

### Where did the workers come from?

**Question 1:** Weaker pupils may simply list men, women and children. The stronger will pick out the examples in the sources and text: the poor and unemployed in the Highlands and Islands of Scotland, and orphans in the care of local authorities. Source 1 also illustrates the wide range of skilled workers required to run a factory mill – not just weavers, but people skilled in wheel making, etc.

The mills at New Lanark are pictured in Source 5 on pages 20–21.

**Source 2:** 'wrote' is not a typographical error, but acceptable grammatical practice in the eighteenth and early nineteenth centuries.

### How were the child workers treated?

**Question 1:** The dangers shown in Sources 4–8 include being beaten, carrying heavy and bulky loads, getting limbs or clothes caught in unprotected machinery, tiredness, having to crawl under machines, etc.

**Source 5:** If you look carefully, you can see evidence that the engraving has been 'doctored'. Both the adult in the foreground and the adult in the background (right) seem to have a 'third arm' raised, ready to beat the child(ren) with a stick; the man in the foreground appears to be holding the child with his left hand. When and why the doctoring took place would be an interesting discussion point in class although we have not been able as yet to ascertain any details. It is most likely, however, that this was a 'moderation' necessary for the original publication.

Comparisons between these conditions and those of today could lead into a fruitful discussion on health and safety at work, which not only contributes to the cross-curricular theme of Health Education, but is also an important element of Economic and Industrial Understanding.

(Pages 18–19)

**Sources 10 and 11:** *The Memoir of Robert Blincoe* is published in a number of editions, and should still be available through your library. Question 1 refers to these two sources.

**Sources 13 and 14**, with their question and answer format, should ideally be read out in class.

**Activity:** Sources 4–17 are very vivid. As an alternative activity, pupils could use these sources to plan and present a TV documentary exposing conditions in the factories.

### ENQUIRY: ROBERT OWEN: A BETTER WAY TO RUN A FACTORY?

Pupils' Book pp. 20–21
Worksheets 5, 6

On pages 12–15, pupils learned about Richard Arkwright as a successful businessman, and discussed the qualities that made him successful. In this enquiry, Robert Owen's approach to business is compared with Arkwright's. Owen successfully ran a large factory and made profits, but his thinking about society in general was different from and more highly developed than Arkwright's.

The focus in this single-spread enquiry is on Owen's theories for running a successful business. It raises key questions about the nature of business, which are still relevant and important today, and which allow more work to be done on Economic and Industrial Understanding, as well as on Citizenship.

It also forms a useful base for later examinations of the union movement in Section 6.

#### Could Robert Owen's ideas work?

**Worksheet 5:** This is an extension exercise for more able pupils. It uses some difficult source material to look more deeply at Owen's ideas.

**Summary questions 1–3: Worksheet 6** provides support for pupils.

### ENQUIRY: BOULTON AND WATT: WHO WAS MORE IMPORTANT?

Pupils' Book pp. 22–25
Worksheets 2, 7

Behind many businesses lay a partnership. In this two-spread enquiry we look at one very famous partnership between an inventor (James Watt) and an entrepreneur (Matthew Boulton). The enquiry is intended to convey the dynamics of the partnership; the picture strip which forms the heart of the enquiry picks out the main events in the story. It also suggests the different contribution to the partnership made by each of the men. The hope is that pupils will be able to identify and evaluate the contribution of each of the two men (and also the contribution of others such as Boulton's foreman).

(Pages 22–23)

**Sources 1–3:** Unusually, there are questions hidden in the text: pupils are being asked to find out all they can about the Soho Works. These questions are intended for class discussion and require detailed interrogation of the sources. Don't forget the information given in the caption to Source 1.

In Source 3 you can just see the four courtyards of the Manufactory, as mentioned in Source 2, at the top right. You can also see in Source 3 the mill pond, the main road (a mail route, down which stagecoaches would pass regularly) and nearby the beginnings of the town, a source of labour.

(Pages 24–25)

#### How did Matthew Boulton work?

**Question 2:** You will need **Worksheet 2** here again – but for the last time.

**Activity:** This allows pupils to reach their own conclusions about the whole of Section 2. Worksheet 2 – filled out – will be a useful preparation for the Activity.

If Madame Tussaud's is within easy travelling distance of the school, it is well worth a visit. The waxworks are, of course, twentieth-century presentations and interpretations of individuals from the past. You can discuss which figures the exhibitors have chosen to include and which to exclude from the exhibition, or analyse how individuals are presented and what impression this presentation gives.

**Worksheet 7:** This provides an opportunity for emphasising aspects of Economic and Industrial Understanding. Pupils choose one option for each question and then work out their score using the system below.

Scoring for Worksheet 7: we've given three points for what we consider to be the best idea in the context of nineteenth-century business, and one for the worst. These questions are not intended to have right and wrong answers, and you might disagree with our scoring.

For question 4 we've scored two options as 'equal best'. Our suggestions are:
**Q1:** a=2, b=3, c=1
**Q2:** a=1, b=2, c=3
**Q3:** a=1, b=3, c=2
**Q4:** a=1, b=3, c=3
**Q5:** a=2, b=3, c=1
**Q6:** a=2, b=3, c=1

It is equally possible to use this worksheet as a basis for class discussion: for each question put the answers in an order of priority, then compare your order with ours.

**Worksheet 14:** Section 2 may have given the impression that all entrepreneurs were male. Most of the best known were, but Worksheet 14 introduces one who was a woman – Charlotte Guest.

## Section 3: What caused the Industrial Revolution?

In Section 2 – without using the term once – we examined the 'industrial revolution' in practice: the new entrepreneurs, the new industries, the new machines, the new methods of work. Now it is time to use the term Industrial Revolution overtly, as we move on to examine systematically some of the factors that caused industrial change in the period 1750–1900.

We have chosen to deal in Section 3 with four main factors: agricultural change, raw materials, improvements in transport and the growth of trade and Empire. Remember that in Section 2 pupils have already encountered other factors, notably the contribution of individuals and the entrepreneurial spirit, and the importance of new technology.

The main aim of this third section is to show that we cannot explain the Industrial Revolution simply as the result of the activities of a few inventors and entrepreneurs. There are, after all, enterprising people in every generation. The important question is why businessmen and women were particularly successful in the period 1750–1900. You will need to make an appropriate link here: 'Of course the Industrial Revolution was more than a few clever businessmen. . . let's see what else was important.'

The ordering of the enquiries in Section 3 is conventional, but throughout the section one is faced by a chicken and egg problem. The development of British industry was clearly not linear and its causes were anything but. However, in order to make the material accessible to pupils it is necessary to examine each factor in turn. Only once this has been completed is it possible to stress the connections between the factors, and these are endless. This is made clear in the final enquiry on pages 46–47.

## ENQUIRY: HOW DID FARMERS PRODUCE MORE FOOD?

Pupils' Book pp. 26–29
Worksheet 8

Before setting out on this enquiry, it is important that you put Section 3 into context for pupils.

Firstly, ensure that pupils are clear about the term Industrial Revolution. They have already studied political revolutions, such as the English Revolution (and the French Revolution if you used *Societies in Change*). The economic and social changes we have touched on in Section 2 were so great that people have compared them to these great political revolutions and called them the Industrial Revolution. So one of the questions we will be addressing is whether the changes were really great enough to justify that term.

Secondly, remind pupils that they have already seen some reasons for these changes. Now we are going to look at a range of other factors.

The noteworthy achievement of producing more food while at the same time using less labour was essential for the progress of the Industrial Revolution. Large numbers of people working in towns could not be self-sufficient in food, and large amounts of surplus food had to be produced to feed them.

This two-spread enquiry looks briefly at the ways in which agriculture developed during the late eighteenth and early nineteenth centuries. It is important to stress that in this period we are just as likely to find inventors

and entrepreneurs in farming as we are in industry. In fact, it was during this period that farming became an industry, with farmers like Coke sharing the attitudes of the entrepreneurs we have already studied.

(Pages 26–27)

## Farming in 1750

**Source 1:** It is important to emphasise that the reconstruction drawing of part of the Norfolk village of Ashill in 1750 is an artist's impression. The available evidence has been interpreted to convey a feeling for what the village would have been like at this time.

**Question 1:** If support is needed for this question you can get groups of pupils to look for specific problems, e.g. anything that shows land was wasted, any features which would make it difficult to introduce new farming ideas, etc.

The cards from **Worksheet 8** can also be used here if you wish. Split the class into nine groups. Give each group a 'Problem' card, and ask the pupils to say why this problem might prevent increases in food production.

### Enclosure in Ashill

This theme is picked up again on pages 52–55.

(Pages 28–29)

## Changes

**Questions 1 and 2: Worksheet 8** is a support exercise for these two questions, which can also be used for homework.

Cut out the 'Problem' cards, which are based on the boxes around Source 1 on the previous page, and the 'Change' cards, which are based on Source 4.

The cards can then be used in a number of ways.

■ The simplest is matching problem to change – though it is not a strict one-to-one matching exercise. A number of change cards can be linked to a single problem and vice versa.

■ Another possibility is for one half of the class to rank the problems in order of severity, and the other half to rank the changes in order of importance.

■ The cards can also be used as the basis for a class display. On one panel use the 'Problem' cards with pictures and explanations to illustrate the problems at the start of the period. On another panel do the same for the changes.

### Case study: Thomas Coke

This case study of Thomas Coke has been designed to allow pupils to investigate different interpretations of Coke. They may need to be taken through Sources 7–11 carefully – they are quite difficult.

### Who improved Holkham?

It was not only in his day that Coke was regarded as the architect of the success at Holkham. The following source, written in 1912, sums up the view most people would have held until well into this century. You could read it out to the class to set the scene for Source 11.

---

Written in 1912 by Lord Ernle in *English Farming Past and Present*

*"The annual rental of Holkham rose from £2200 in 1776 to £20,000 in 1816.*

*When Coke took his land in hand, not an acre of wheat was to be seen. The thin sandy soil produced but a scanty yield of rye. Naturally wanting in richness, it was still further impoverished by a barbarous system of cropping... Coke determined to grow wheat. He marled and clayed the land, purchased large quantities of manure, drilled his wheat and turnips, grew sainfoin and clover, trebled his livestock...*

*His efforts were not confined to the home farm. Early and late he worked in his smock frock, assisting tenants to improve their stocks and herds... He tested every novelty himself, and offered to his neighbours only the results of his own successful experiments.*

*His farm buildings, dwelling-houses, and cottages were models to other landlords. By offering long leases of 21 years, he guaranteed to improving farmers a return for their energy and outlay..."*

---

**Questions 1 and 2** could be discussed in class. For question 2 you may need to point pupils back to Sources 8 and 11.

## ENQUIRY: DID BRITAIN HAVE THE RAW MATERIALS IT NEEDED?

Pupils' Book pp. 30–31

This is a single-spread enquiry. There is scope for cross-curricular work with the Geography department (as indeed there is in the subsequent enquiries on transport).

**Source 1:** We have had to be selective – we cannot show all Britain's raw materials. We have, instead, picked out those that figure most prominently in the Industrial Revolution. It is also impossible to show all the sources of those raw materials on a single map. If we have left out details of your local region, you can begin by correcting this. Get pupils to work with a local map to draw up an inventory of the raw materials available in the locality. This can be profitably done as cross-curricular work with the Geography department.

N.B. Pig iron is the name for the ingots obtained by smelting (see Source 2 on page 10).

If you can obtain samples of each raw material for the pupils to see and handle, this can provide an excellent opportunity to consider the difficulties of extracting, gathering, transporting or handling raw materials.

**Source 2:** We have chosen a range of objects to show different uses of coal, iron, cotton and other textiles, china clay, etc.

You would do even better to bring some nineteenth-century objects into the classroom. Pupils may be able to do this themselves – perhaps going back to the material they brought in or wrote about for questions 1 and 2 on page 9.

**Question 2:** Pupils can work in groups, researching one object at a time. They can answer questions such as what each object is made of, what raw materials might have been used in its manufacture (e.g. coal to fire furnaces), what they think it was used for, what type of person would have used it, whether they think it normally lasted for a long time, whether we use the same thing or something different today. (There is an excellent booklet, *Learning from Objects*, published by English Heritage which contains many ideas for using artefacts in the classroom.)

We have deliberately left the captions in Source 2 very open to encourage the pupils to think hard about each object. But to save you some research, we have been able to find out the following details.

■ Iron fountain: probably made at Coalbrookdale. Main raw materials: coal, iron ore and limestone. Refer pupils back to page 10 for iron making.

■ China plate: this contains some fascinating information about the Empire, and is a typical example of Victorian souvenir pottery. The Latin motto translates as 'Where there is virtue, there is Victoria'. Main raw materials: clay, china clay, coal.

■ Clothes: summer fashions for 1838, a view in Windsor Park. Main raw materials: wool, cotton, silk, etc.

■ Locomotive: Stephenson's *North Star*, built in 1837. Main raw materials: pig iron, coal, timber.

■ Post box: this is a hexagonal cast iron post box of a design first introduced in 1866. These were made in Dudley in the Midlands and were the standard design until 1879. This was also, coincidentally, the period in which the pillar box colour was standardised to red. Main raw materials: iron, coal, limestone.

## ENQUIRY: DID TRANSPORT NEED IMPROVING?

Pupils' Book pp. 32–33
Worksheet 9

Pupils will probably have concluded from the previous spread that Britain had an abundant supply of raw materials, yet they were clearly not always in the right place.

This single-spread enquiry sets up a series of in-depth

case studies of nineteenth-century transport improvements by looking at the state of British transport at the beginning of the period. The case study approach has been chosen deliberately, but its danger is that pupils do not see the overall picture. Note, therefore, that on pages 40–41 there is a survey of overall transport developments during this period.

## Road transport in 1750

Those pupils who studied the Medieval Realms unit in this series will have had a very thorough grounding in road transport in the Middle Ages. As the text points out, by 1750, with the increase in traffic, the roads were in many ways in a worse state than they had been 300 or more years before.

## How were roads improved?

It would be useful to find out details of your local turnpikes and of journey times to neighbouring cities. You may even be able to get a local equivalent of Source 6 from your county archives office.

**Source 7:** Note the camber to provide drainage, and the two layers of compacted stone to provide good foundations.

**Worksheet 9** shows the effect that improved travel times had in 'shrinking' Britain. It is designed to be independent, so can be used as homework. If you make colour versions of these maps on transparent overlays you can present the data with greater impact. You can add a twelve-hour isoline and a 36-hour isoline from the information given. You could also add a twelve-hour isoline for today.

## ENQUIRY: WHY WAS THE BRIDGEWATER CANAL BUILT?

Pupils' Book pp. 34–35

It is far more useful to study in depth the building of a single canal in a particular area than to tell the whole story of canal building in a superficial way. This single-spread enquiry considers why a canal was needed in the Liverpool and Manchester area, how the canal was built, and the consequences of building the canal. All of these questions have been set in the context of the industrial needs within the locality at the time.

## The problem

**Source 1:** This shows the transport situation in 1750, with only the existing roads. It is built on in Source 1 on page 36 and Source 6 on page 39. It might be worth having one big map of the area to hand to support the work on each source.

## The solution: the Bridgewater Canal

**Source 3** contains a great deal of information. You may wish to help pupils make sense of it by writing each

paragraph on a separate piece of card and handing a set of cards to each pair of pupils. They can then sort the cards for question 1.

You may think that we have not given Brindley much credit in Source 3. Modern research, however, clearly shows that Brindley's role was limited and that his reputation as the leading canal engineer of the age rests on his involvement in the building of later canals. The Bridgewater Canal was designed by the Duke himself and his land agent, John Gilbert; Brindley was brought in at a later stage to give practical advice on its construction. In fact, Brindley was not involved at all in the extension of the canal underground; the credit for this should go to John Gilbert.

This information makes questions 1 and 2 particularly important. For work on historical interpretations it should be possible to see what other textbooks say about Brindley's role. Many of them give Brindley all the credit: e.g. 'The canal was opened in 1761 and included a tunnel and the Barton aqueduct over the River Irwell. It was built by James Brindley.' (*The Industrial Revolution*, R. Unwin, 1980.) What impression does this give of Brindley's contribution? How accurate is it?

## The results

**Activity:** Encourage pupils to use the source material and information on pages 32–35 to prepare their poster, and to make it a poster suitable for the time.

## ENQUIRY: HOW WAS THE LIVERPOOL AND MANCHESTER RAILWAY BUILT?

Pupils' Book pp. 36–39
Worksheets 10, 11

This two-spread enquiry follows on naturally from the previous spread. As very soon becomes clear on page 36, the Bridgewater Canal did not solve the area's transport problems for long.

There are three main points to be stressed about the building of the Liverpool and Manchester Railway:

■ It was a business enterprise similar to many of the others already studied. Much detail is included about the financing and running of the company.
■ There were many practical engineering difficulties in building the railway which had to be overcome.
■ The railway had an enormous impact.

(Pages 36–37)

## The problem

**Activity:** To prepare for this have a class brainstorm of the problems implied by the annotation to Source 1.
**Worksheet 10** provides a possible structure for pupils' work.

## The solution: the Liverpool and Manchester Railway

**Stages 2 and 3:** This could be used to introduce some cross-curricular work with Geography colleagues. There may be a recent local dispute over a new road or development which has been studied in Geography. A comparison could be made between the procedures involved in approving a development then and today.

(Pages 38–39)

## Building the railway

The diagram below shows the profile of the railway. N.B. The gradients are obviously exaggerated for the purposes of the diagram. Even so, 1 in 48 is *very* steep for a railway.

You can see from Source 13 on page 5 that the opening of a railway was a great spectator event. The story of the opening of the Liverpool and Manchester Railway is a memorable one which you may wish to tell your pupils. Here are some of the details.

The opening was on 13 September 1830. So many people gathered in the two cities that it was impossible to find eating space or accommodation in either city.

The first trains ran from Liverpool to Manchester. Grandstands were built for people to sit and watch the beginning of the journey. The crowds extended along both sides of the line for eight miles beyond the city. There were many distinguished guests there, including the Duke of Wellington (the Prime Minister) and other members of the government, all of whom travelled in one of the trains.

There were seven trains in all. They travelled the seventeen miles to Parkside, where they stopped to take on water and fuel. Some of the passengers got out and walked along the track, exchanging greetings with their friends in the other carriages. This group included one of the government ministers, William Huskisson.

Just as Huskisson was shaking hands with Wellington, who was in a carriage, the *Rocket* appeared. The crowd of people on the line scattered quickly, but Huskisson was one of the last to move. He ran first to one side of the track, but could not climb the steep bank. He retraced his steps, apparently hoping to climb into the carriage. He tried to do so, but missed his footing and fell to the ground. His left leg fell across the near rail and although the driver of the *Rocket* made every effort to stop his engine, the wheels of the engine and several carriages ran over Huskisson's thigh and lower leg, fracturing them.

He was carried to a nearby house, where it was decided not to amputate the leg. The bones of the lower leg had been broken into small pieces. The thigh had been broken into several fragments, and the muscles had been mangled. Huskisson died later that evening.

### Was the railway a success?

**Question 1: Worksheet 11** provides extension material on reactions to the railway to help pupils answer this question in greater depth. Source 8 and the question are reproduced on the worksheet to make it self-contained so that it can be used for homework.

## *ENQUIRY: CHANGING TRANSPORT*

Pupils' Book pp.40–41
Worksheet 9

This single-spread enquiry is designed to ensure that pupils have an overview of the main transport developments during this period.

### New roads

See **Worksheet 9** for a map version of these journey time statistics.

### New railways

There is an in-depth study of the growth of one seaside resort, Brighton, on pages 60–63.

**Activity:** Pupils will need a blank map of Britain on which to mark their route.

## *ENQUIRY: EMPIRE AND TRADE*

Pupils' Book pp. 42–45

It is not usual for Britain's trade to be considered primarily through the slave trade, but as this two-spread enquiry makes clear the slave trade formed the most significant part of Britain's eighteenth-century trade. Other types of trade are dealt with briefly on page 45.

The debate over how far the slave trade contributed to the Industrial Revolution still rages, but this is no reason not to involve pupils in it. If further reading for

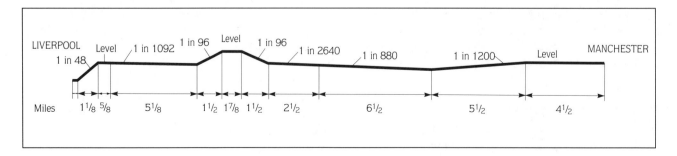

the teacher is required on this topic, Eric Williams' *From Columbus to Castro: The History of the Caribbean 1492–1969* is recommended.

The themes of slavery and the slave trade are picked up again later, on pages 70–75, *Were the British racist?* and pages 80–85, *Why was slavery abolished?* These enquiries could all be taught together as one depth study.

(Pages 42–43)

As **Source 1** shows, Britain's Empire in 1800 was still relatively small: Australia was annexed in 1823, and large-scale colonisation of Africa did not occur until as late as the 1880s.

(Pages 43–44)

### Industrial expansion and the slave trade

The cities of Bristol and Liverpool are used as examples here, but depending on where you live it might be possible to find local examples of buildings or institutions that were founded on slave trade profits.

(Page 45)

### Why did London need new docks?

The aim here is to broaden the picture slightly to show a range of British imports. But the page is fairly self-contained and can be used flexibly. For example, it can be used alongside the enquiry on raw materials on pages 30–31.

## ENQUIRY: WHY THERE AND WHY THEN?

Pupils' Book pp. 46–47

This single-spread enquiry rounds off much of the work covered by the unit so far.

The main objectives are:
■ to show that there were a number of factors causing the Industrial Revolution to happen when and where it did
■ to show that no single factor is an adequate explanation in itself and that the connections between the factors are very important. It is only when we put all these factors together that we begin to get an answer to the question 'Why there and why then?'
■ to show that each factor is in itself problematic, and that there is a case to be made for and against each factor. This begins to make it clear why historians can disagree about the causes of the Industrial Revolution.

**Question 2:** Pupils may need help with question 2. It might be a good idea to draw an example of a flow diagram on the board. You might also wish to write out the key statements on cards for pupils to stick down on the page to make their flow diagram.

**Question 4:** This is a key piece of work that will

show pupils' grasp of a wide range of issues. Some pupils may need your help in structuring their answer. For example:
*Paragraph 1:* start with a general introduction saying what we mean by the 'Industrial Revolution'.
*Paragraph 2:* summarise briefly the range of factors that helped cause it.
*Paragraphs 3 and 4:* choose one factor and explain in detail how it helped cause the Industrial Revolution.
*Paragraph 5:* write a conclusion saying what you think was the most important factor.

## ENQUIRY: WAS THERE AN INDUSTRIAL REVOLUTION?

Pupils' Book pp. 48–49

This is a single-spread enquiry, which raises important issues regarding the Industrial Revolution. Was there really a 'revolution'? If there was, what was it? Did it affect all industries in the same way and at the same rate? Were there any threads of continuity between pre-revolution and post-revolution industry?

The Domestic System is examined first; we can then consider whether the change from Domestic System to Factory System was a total change or whether there was some continuity. The second part of the enquiry briefly considers those industries that retained the Domestic System until very late in the period.

### Did the factory system take over?

**Question 1:** Source 7 – brickfields in the Midlands; Source 8 – a rope making factory; Source 9 – brush making in the East End of London. Pupils will need to look very closely to puzzle out what is going on.

**Activity:** The activity focuses on change and continuity, but you may well also want to use the opportunity to explore the concept of 'revolution'. How far do these changes constitute a 'revolution', and how does it differ from revolutions already studied, e.g. the English Revolution in the seventeenth century, the scientific revolution in the eighteenth century or the French Revolution?

## Section 4: Was life getting better?

After looking at the nature of the Industrial Revolution and its causes, we now move on to its consequences, in particular its effects on people, both individuals and communities.

This is done through a variety of case studies. First, we consider how two actual families were affected during the period, then how life in the countryside in general changed. We then concentrate on two specific and contrasting towns: Merthyr Tydfil, an industrial town, and Brighton, a seaside resort. The questions underlying each of these enquiries are 'How much did life change?' and 'Were the changes for the better?'

## ENQUIRY: THE STORY OF TWO FAMILIES

Pupils' Book pp. 50–51
Worksheets 12, 13

This is a single-spread enquiry based on research into the family history of two real families. Some schools have found that this spread works well as an introductory overview for the unit as a whole.

**Activity:** Before you begin to study the Eyles and the Glovers, you might want to make much more of this activity, which serves as an introduction to the ideas on which we will be focusing throughout Section 4. You can use **Worksheet 12** as an alternative or an extension to the Activity.

The aim of both the Activity and the worksheet is for pupils to establish some criteria by which quality of life in the past can be measured. This is worth discussing in class. Even in a fairly homogenous group, pupils often have very different ideas about what is important.

After some initial discussion in the whole class, let them brainstorm some ideas in groups. These could then be compared with the list on Worksheet 12.

The story of the Glovers and the Eyles is based on research carried out by the granddaughter of Charles Herbert Glover and Emily Eyles.

It shows many patterns that are typical of the changes in the period. But even more important is the fact that these two families do not always conform to the 'norm' for the period. For example, although in general life expectancy in Britain increased between the beginning and the end of the nineteenth century, this is not always reflected in these families: Matthew Glover, born in 1780, lived to be 78; Charles Herbert Glover, born in 1850, lived to be 56. Real living people do not conform to statistical averages. This is an important lesson for pupils to learn.

However, you could discuss with the class the extent to which these families do appear to be 'typical' – their story contains some important trends typical of successful middle-class families during this period.

**Questions 1–6** take pupils quite successfully into the information about the families, but you may like to use other approaches that suit your pupils.

■ It might help some pupils if a family tree is drawn on the board. Or you could ask them to attempt a family tree and see how they do.

■ You could begin by getting pupils to think about their own family histories. See if they can go back as far as their grandparents and record similar information: names, age at marriage, age when died, number of children, occupations. These could then be compared with the Glovers and Eyles.

**Question 1:** to save you working all this out, the figures are:

| | Age at marriage | Age at death | No. of children |
|---|---|---|---|
| Matthew Glover<br>Ann Wood | 26<br>23 | 78<br>63 | 4 |
| Matthew Henry Glover<br>Elizabeth Barker | 31<br>26 | 67<br>c.43 | 6 |
| Charles Herbert Glover<br>Emily Eyles | 37<br>33 | 56<br>61 | 3 |
| Hope Eyles<br>Jane Gibson | 22<br>21 | 68<br>c.67 | 6 |
| Samuel Eyles<br>Matilda Ann Marsh | 24<br>24 | 70<br>63 | 12 |

**Worksheet 13** is a map-based exercise to support question 3.

**Question 4:**

■ Matthew Glover (and his father): butcher.

■ Matthew Henry Glover: apprentice draper, later draper owning his own shop, then woollen manufacturer, then owned an engineering and machine making firm.

■ Elizabeth Barker's father: farmer.

■ Charles Herbert Glover: ran with his brother their timber import and sawmill business.

■ Hope Eyles: freestone mason, later master baker, later carrier.

■ Jane Eyles: straw bonnet maker.

■ Samuel Eyles: wheelwright and coach builder, later owned his own coach making business, later travelling salesman.

■ Marsh family: market gardeners.

■ Emily Eyles: paid companion.

## ENQUIRY: DID LIFE IN THE COUNTRYSIDE GET BETTER?

Pupils' Book pp. 52–55

This two-spread enquiry is both a case study of the village of Ashill (which pupils have already studied on pages 26–29), and a more general study of developments in agricultural areas in lowland Britain.

The main focus is on the nature of change in rural communities between 1750 and 1900, and to a lesser extent on the reconstruction of rural community life in the late eighteenth and nineteenth centuries. The enquiry also examines the consequences of parliamentary enclosure.

There are a number of possibilities for extension work on this topic if you wish to develop it as a depth study. One of the most interesting and challenging would be to work on 'interpretations' in a study of images of the countryside. You can gather different perceptions of country life in Victorian times and compare them with the realities of life in farming communities investigated in this enquiry. For example, paintings such as Sir George Clausen's *The Stone Pickers* (in the Laing Art Gallery, Newcastle), or Birket Foster's *A Cottage at Hambledon* (in the Tate Gallery, London) can be placed alongside poetry by William Morris or George Meredith and prose such as Thomas Hardy's – or film adaptations of his novels, e.g. *Far From the Madding Crowd*.

It might also be possible to study a village in your locality. Local societies often produce 'village histories', and school logbooks can provide pupils with some fascinating work.

(Pages 52–53)

## Life in the village before 1850

**Source 1:** This is a close-up of the central area of the village as shown in Source 1 on page 26.

**Question 2:** This could be used as a class discussion.

## Hard Times

If you used *Societies in Change*, the Y8 textbook in this series, the wars with France will need no explanation. If you didn't, you might! Note also that another result of the wars was the growth and success of the South Wales iron industry (see the Merthyr Tydfil enquiry, page 56).

(Pages 54–55)

## Did life get better after 1850?

**Activity:** Have some postcard-size cards available.

**Questions 4–7** should be tackled before the Activity. For question 4, pupils should be directed back to Source 2 to make their comparison. **Questions 5–7** are more complex than they first appear, and can cover as much of the enquiry as pupils are capable of tackling in one go. They may also find it useful to go back to Source 1 on page 26.

## *ENQUIRY: HOW DID MERTHYR TYDFIL CHANGE?*

Pupils' Book pp. 56–59
Worksheets 14, 15

This two-spread enquiry provides a deliberate contrast to the previous enquiry. In rural Ashill change was only gradual. In Merthyr Tydfil, an industrial and urban community, the pace of change during the eighteenth and nineteenth centuries was rapid. The case study also helps to bring a Welsh dimension into pupils' work.

The Merthyr iron industry is also notable for the important role played by one of the least typical entrepreneurs of the century, Lady Charlotte Guest, who for a time ran the Dowlais iron works. **Worksheet 14** is

an extension worksheet devoted to exploring the role and working methods of Charlotte Guest.

Whereas in the previous enquiry pupils had some prior knowledge of Ashill on which to build their investigation, in this enquiry they are coming to the subject matter cold. It might therefore be worth our laying out in some detail the background to the Merthyr iron industry for you to use at your discretion.

## Growth

Ironstone and limestone were quarried in the area, and in the early days charcoal from the local woodlands was used to smelt iron. However, as Merthyr stands on the northern part of the South Wales coalfield, when coke smelting was developed the local iron industry was well placed to use the new fuel. Water power, to drive bellows and forge hammers, was also readily available in the area.

The four main iron works in Merthyr (Dowlais, Cyfartha, Penydarren and Plymouth) were all set up in the 1750s and 1760s, when the demand for iron was high owing to the Seven Years' War. Dowlais and Cyfartha were the biggest.

Dowlais was bought by John Guest. His grandson, Josiah John Guest, took the works over in 1807 and made it into the largest iron works in the world at the time. When he became ill and then died (in 1852), the management of the works was taken over by his wife, Lady Charlotte Guest (see Worksheet 14).

Richard Crawshay acquired the Cyfartha works in 1783. In 1810, his grandson William Crawshay II took over the management of the company. In 1825, from some of the profits, he built himself a grand mansion, Cyfartha Castle, on a hillside overlooking his works.

The iron industry in Merthyr grew rapidly. The number of blast furnaces in the town increased as follows:

| Year | Number of blast furnaces |
| --- | --- |
| 1784 | 4 |
| 1812 | 18 |
| 1850 | 41 |

The blast furnaces produced pig iron. Much of this was converted into bar iron, using the 'puddling' process, also known as the 'Welsh method'. The puddled iron was hammered and then passed through rollers to produce bars and rails.

### Reasons for growth

Rails for railways were one of the most important products of the Merthyr iron industry. The Dowlais works supplied rails for the Liverpool and Manchester Railway, and also exported rails all over Europe and to other parts of the world. Many of the railways in Russia had rails which were made at Dowlais.

The growth of the iron industry was helped by improvements in transport. The road from Merthyr to

Cardiff had been very poor, but was improved when a turnpike trust was formed in 1771. In 1794, the Glamorganshire Canal linked Merthyr with the docks at Cardiff. The owners of the four main iron works were all shareholders. Richard Crawshay was the biggest shareholder, and so the canal went right up to his works. The other ironmasters built a tramway to link their works to the canal. This was completed in 1802. In 1804, a steam locomotive built by Richard Trevithick hauled five wagons and a coach along the ten miles from Penydarren iron works to the canal – the first steam train in the world. Later (in 1841), a railway was built all the way from Merthyr to Cardiff.

The ironmasters also owned coal mines in the Merthyr area. They built houses for their skilled workers. Large numbers of workers were attracted to Merthyr from other parts of Wales. Irish, English and Jewish people also came to the town to find employment. Merthyr's population grew rapidly – from 7705 in 1801 (much larger than it had been 50 years before) to 17,404 in 1821 and 46,382 in 1851.

### Decline

By the mid-nineteenth century, however, problems were developing. The local ironstone was running out, and so this vital raw material had to be imported from other parts of Britain and from abroad. The invention of the converter by Henry Bessemer in 1856 made possible the production of cheap steel in large quantities. Steel is stronger than iron, and therefore preferable for most purposes. New steel industries developed in parts of Britain where more plentiful iron ore was available (e.g. Northamptonshire and Cleveland). At Dowlais, there was a major investment to make steel production possible; the other iron works, however, gradually shut down. Coal mining continued, and increasing quantities of coal were sent down the railway to Cardiff and exported to other parts of Britain and the world. But Merthyr's golden age was over.

(Pages 56–57)

### People at work in the Merthyr iron works

**Sources 7, 8 and 10** show aspects of the production process described in the written sources.

**Question 3: Worksheet 15** provides further information about various jobs in the Merthyr iron industry and what they involved.

(Pages 58–59)

### Housing and health

**Sources 14 and 15:** The reconstructed cottages at the Welsh Folk Museum can be investigated as historical interpretations. Questions 8 and 9 touch on this subject, but there is scope to develop it, especially in class discussion. It is important that pupils are aware that reconstructions such as these, or any museum exhibits, are as much interpretations of the past as, for example,

the views of a historian about whether life was getting better in the nineteenth century. The way a museum displays, selects and describes its exhibits is in itself an interpretation, which needs to be examined and questioned.

**Question 2:** Top is 1895, centre 1855 and bottom 1805.

## ENQUIRY: BESIDE THE SEASIDE!

Pupils' Book pp. 60–63
Worksheet 16

In this two-spread enquiry Brighton is used as a case study of the growth and development of a seaside holiday resort.

Two related issues are central to this enquiry:
■ How did Brighton change between 1750 and 1900? What factors caused these changes, and were they changes for the better?
■ What do the changes in Brighton tell us about changing patterns of leisure and quality of life in Britain generally?

Although Brighton was one of the largest and most successful resorts throughout this period, similar trends can be seen in the development of many other towns around the coastline. If your school is close to a seaside town such as Margate, Southend, Great Yarmouth, Skegness, Scarborough, Blackpool, Llandudno, Weston-Super-Mare, Torquay, Weymouth or Bournemouth you could use local history sources to investigate similarities and differences to the story of Brighton. You can also use such local work to help pupils reconstruct what a nineteenth-century seaside holiday was really like, and how it compares with today.

This enquiry also includes a case study of Sake Deen Mahomed, whose baths were a major attraction in early nineteenth-century Brighton. It provides an opportunity to focus on the contribution of ethnic minorities to life in Britain before 1900. This theme is developed further on pages 75 and 82. For more on this theme in general, and Sake Deen Mahomed in particular, see Rosina Visram's book *Ayahs, Lascars and Princes*.

(Pages 60–61)

### Changes: 1750–1900

**Question 1: Worksheet 16** reproduces the 1779 and 1824 maps from Source 2 so that the exercise is self standing for homework purposes. Page 2 of the worksheet takes this exercise a stage further, including an 1880 map for comparison.

Note the following changes in particular between 1779 and 1824: the increased size of the town, the closely packed new housing to the east of the Steyne (Kemp Town), the parks, the development along the seashore to the west, the King's Road, the pier, the Pavilion (Palace), the fish market where the battery once was, the windmills, etc.

## Sake Deen Mahomed

Discuss Source 1 in detail with pupils before starting this section. We have got a little used to images of the Royal Pavilion by now, so draw pupils' attention to the contrast between the elaborate style of the palace and the simple terraces of Kemp Town on the right.

Shampoo is actually an Indian word – Hindi for massage – and one of the many loan words that have travelled from the Indian subcontinent and into the English language. Bungalow, juggernaut, pundit, curry, verandah, thug and bangle are others. Loan words illustrate historical links between countries and serve to remind us of the types of things that one culture borrows from another.

**Question 2:** As the text explains, racial prejudice was certainly one problem. This is worth discussing at this point, although the main discussion of nineteenth-century racism is not undertaken until pages 70–75.

(Pages 61–62)

## Brighton as an upper-class resort

**Source 8:** Bathing was subject to an increasingly stringent set of bye-laws in some resorts – see, for example, the bathing bye-laws for Cromer in Norfolk (Source 10 on page 67).

(Pages 62–63)

## Brighton as a popular resort

**Source 12: Worksheet 16** includes a map of Brighton in 1880, showing many of these features and others associated with the holiday industry such as the railway station or the race course. It can be used as a homework exercise or to support classroom work on this spread.

**Question 3:** All too often stories of seaside towns focus exclusively on the experience of the tourists, missing out those who lived in the town all year round. This question is intended to provoke a more rounded classroom discussion. If Brighton got better, for whom did it get better – the tourists or the residents or both? The maps on Worksheet 16 will be useful here as well.

# Section 5: Victorian values

This section investigates an important topic, and one which has recently generated much controversy. The enquiries focus on the ideas, beliefs and attitudes of the Victorians, but there is also much scope here for work on historical interpretations, particularly in the first enquiry.

The first enquiry, *What are Victorian values?*, aims to set the scene. The subsequent enquiries, *Were the British racist?*, *Did the Victorians care?* and *The Victorians and women workers*, develop pupils' understanding of Victorian values by taking three themes and investigating them in depth. All pupils should tackle the first enquiry, but for the other three it

would be possible for your class to split into three study groups, each tackling one enquiry.

(With thanks to Jenny and Martin Tucker for ideas and material used in this section.)

## *ENQUIRY: WHAT ARE VICTORIAN VALUES?*

Pupils' Book pp. 64–69
Worksheets 17, 18

This three-spread enquiry begins by looking at the debate about Victorian values which ran through the early and mid-1980s. The possibilities to develop pupils' understanding of historical interpretations are obvious. *Why* do interpretations differ? *How* do politicians and others use the past to their own ends and to support their own arguments? How does this use of history *affect* the popular view of a period?

The enquiry places an especial emphasis on using visual sources. In particular, pupils are asked to do detailed interrogations of a number of nineteenth-century paintings. You might wish to obtain slides of some of them to use in class.

For most Victorians, Britain's 'expansion, trade and industry' was a cause of celebration. The final pages of this enquiry, therefore, bring pupils back to this idea, which not only lies at the heart of this study unit but is also an essential part of Victorian values.

(Pages 64–65)

**Questions 1–3** are most suitable for class discussion, although after the discussion pupils could write up their own answer to question 3.

**Question 3** is eliciting a provisional judgement only. There has been no systematic evidence as yet for pupils to consider. Rather, they will have gathered *impressions* of the nineteenth century through their study of textile mills and iron works, of industrial towns, rural communities and seaside resorts. The pupils' current impression is a starting point for them to dig deeper and understand more.

## Victorian values

**Sources 2–12**, wittingly or unwittingly, tell us many things about Victorian values.

The discussion of these sources, therefore, needs to take place at two levels: what these sources were intended to tell us about the Victorians, and what they really tell us. We need to go beyond a reading of what the pictures/text show and consider the motivation of the artist/author in creating them.

Some background, and suggested approaches to the illustrations, are given below. All the sources should be fully discussed in class; some of the language in the written sources is quite difficult. Sources 2–12 could also be supplemented by the illustrations in the enquiry *Images of the Victorians* on pages 106–107.

**Source 2:** A painting called *Many Happy Returns of the Day* by W.P.Frith. It shows a Victorian middle-class family celebrating the birthday of one of the children (presumably the one with the wreath) – an idealised portrait of family life with parents, children and grandparents all together. Note the formal dress of the adults and children, the more plainly dressed maid holding the presents, the celebratory wreath, the heavy furnishings, and the gas lights.

**Source 3:** *Work*, a painting by Ford Madox Brown. For detailed notes on this, see **Worksheet 17**.

(Pages 66–67)

**Source 7:** *Kit's Writing Lesson*. The Victorian self help principle idealised! This young man is obviously having difficulty in controlling the pen (from the look of his hands he would seem to be more used to manual labour), but look at his determination. Note the different aspirations implied by the artist for the boy and his sister. He is struggling away at home to improve his handwriting for an office job, while she is getting on with some sewing. Is she envious? Or is it in fact she who is teaching him to write?

Perfect handwriting was essential in those days to obtain an office job. First, 'pothooks', then single letters, then words were practised. The aim was to develop the copperplate style. You could show pupils an example of copperplate and compare it with their own handwriting! It is worth reminding the class that at school Victorian children would probably use slates and pencils. Practice with a pen had to be done at home in the evening. Pupils could also discuss what social class this family might be. How wealthy are they?

**Source 8:** An engraving called *Myself? Or the children?* This is intended to convey the strong ties of family life among the British working classes – but is this an idealised view, simply how the artist would like them to be? The father is shown as respectable and hard-working; possibly on his way home from work just after being paid, he comes across a toy shop – and it is Christmas! Should he spend the money on himself or on his children? It is not difficult to see what the artist thinks he should do. Note that this drawing was published to illustrate a Christmas story. Perhaps the pupils could write the story, or a play, to illustrate Victorian values as part of the Activity on page 67.

**Sources 5, 6 and 12:** These sources clearly show the importance of religious values to the Victorians. We have addressed the issue of religion more directly on **Worksheet 18**. This can be used as extension work or homework here, or better still after the enquiry *The Victorians and women workers* (pages 80–81).

**Activity:** Give pupils some ideas to start off the drama. The best approach is to identify a key phrase or proverb. They must aim to end their drama with this 'moral'. There are plenty of key phrases implied by the sources. For example:

- obey your parents

- put the family first
- work hard
- know your place
- help those less fortunate than yourself.

If pupils need a storyline or situation to build their drama on they could use one of the 'stories' suggested by Sources 2, 3, 7 and 8.

If you can have a discreet video camera at the back of class, try to get a record of the dramas.

(Pages 68–69)

### Expansion, trade and industry: a cause for celebration?

**Source 17:** The exhibits shown include 'moving machines', showing the gears and drive mechanism, furs and skins, a telescope, statues and agricultural machinery.

**Activity:** It would be ideal if pupils could use a DTP system to make their leaflets.

## *ENQUIRY: WERE THE BRITISH RACIST?*

Pupils' Book pp. 70–75

On a number of occasions in this unit so far we have touched on issues of race. In this three-spread enquiry we now try to tackle these issues head on. To do so it is necessary to begin the story further back in the eighteenth century, as the story of slavery is an essential background to nineteenth-century ideas about race.

The enquiry is wide ranging, with many changes of pace. It begins with a story, the case of the slave ship *Zong*, and moves into an analysis of conditions on the slave ships and on the plantations (here the emphasis is on illustrative material and on reconstructing what life was like for the slaves). Finally, against this background, we look specifically at Victorian racial attitudes.

(Pages 70–71)

### The case of the slave ship *Zong*

This is a gruesome story, but one which amply demonstrates some British people's attitudes to slaves. It is probably best if you tell the story to the class in your own words.

(Pages 72–74)

### Slavery on the sugar plantations

**Source 18:** Make it very clear that this photograph shows a black man wearing a neck ring in order to portray with greater intensity the cruelties inflicted on his forebears, and is in no way intended to condone these cruelties or reinforce racial stereotypes.

**Activity:** The intention is to use the full range of material in Sources 11–22 on pages 72–74. To prepare for it the sources should be discussed either in groups or by the class as a whole.

Make it clear that the brochure should not be used just to convey surface information. Values and attitudes should also be conveyed, e.g. what a plantation owner would be proud of, what would be most attractive to prospective buyers.

**Question 3** should prove to be interesting. Some class discussion will be required first. Pupils will also need page references from earlier in the unit – for example, pages 16–19, 48–49, 52–53, 56–59. You will probably have to introduce into the discussion the concept of being 'free', and raise the issue of how important this is compared to other factors, such as health, working conditions and hours, pay, etc.

(Pages 74–75)

## Were the Victorians racist?

The aim here is to focus on Victorian attitudes. As a result, we might seem to be minimising the achievements of blacks. However, both in Mary Seacole on this page and in a subsequent enquiry on the role of black people in the campaign for the abolition of slavery, there are case studies to counter this impression.

There is obvious potential here for work on the cross-curricular theme of Citizenship. For further information about this topic the following books are useful:
*Staying Power of Black People in Britain* by Peter Fryer – very much a book for the teacher rather than the pupil, it contains a wealth of examples and covers the period from the Romans to the 1970s.
*A History of the Black Presence in London*, published by the Greater London Council.
*Black Settlers in Britain* by File and Power.

## ENQUIRY: DID THE VICTORIANS CARE?

Pupils' Book pp.76–79

This two-spread enquiry examines another aspect of Victorian values: attitudes towards and treatment of the poor. The material is divided into two sections: first a general examination of the problem, with a focus on the causes and consequences of the Poor Law Amendment Act, and second a case study of Harriet Kettle, who spent much of her life in institutions such as the workhouse. The study of the life of one real individual can bring home to pupils much about the workhouses and the treatment of the poor that it is difficult for general material to convey.

(Pages 78–79)

**Activity:** The report will be a composite of the many sources provided about different workhouses. Give pupils a structure for their report:
**1.** What are conditions like in the workhouse? Look at

- food
- accommodation
- work.

**2.** What is the workhouse aiming to achieve?
**3.** Is the workhouse succeeding in its aims?
**4.** Do you think anything in either the conditions in the workhouse or its aims needs to be changed?

### The story of Harriet Kettle

**Question 1:** Note the following information which can be pieced together from Sources 15–20:
- For some years between 1851 and 1856 she was a prostitute in Norwich (Source 17)
- On 7 January 1856 she assaulted the master of the workhouse. She was sent to Little Walsingham prison, and stayed there until July 1856, when she was diagnosed as 'a suicidal lunatic' (Sources 16 and 17)
- On 16 July 1856 she was admitted to the County Lunatic Asylum (Source 17)
- By 1858 she was back in the workhouse, and tried to set fire to it on 20 November 1858 (Sources 18 and 19)
- In March 1860 she was sentenced to eighteen months' hard labour for trying to set fire to the workhouse (Source 19)
- On 10 July 1863 she was sent back to the Asylum. She was also physically ill (Source 20).

## ENQUIRY: THE VICTORIANS AND WOMEN WORKERS

Pupils' Book pp.80–81
Worksheet 18

Throughout the Victorian age the momentum of factory reform gathered pace. This single-spread enquiry concludes the work on Victorian values by examining the motives behind legislation on working conditions, in particular as regards women.

The version of history which characterises the factory reformers as kind liberals trying to improve the lot of women is questioned here. Another question which we tackle is whether this legislation actually discriminated against women, in that it took rights away from them which men still enjoyed. It can be argued on the one hand that by this legislation women were being treated as children, or on the other hand that at the time women needed the kind of protection the legislation aimed to provide.

**Question 1:** Possible motives for legislating on women's work revealed in the sources include religious beliefs (Source 2), moral outrage about the treatment of women workers (Source 4), concern about the moral dangers faced by women (Sources 5 and 8), concern about women neglecting their main duty as mother and wife (Sources 6 and 9), the hope that banning women would create more jobs for unemployed men (Sources 7 and 9).

**Activity:** In preparation, discuss the following points:
■ Did these reforms treat women as children?
■ Did they take away from women the right to choose when to work?
■ Did they make women worse off due to lost earnings?
or alternatively:
■ Did these reforms protect women who through poverty and desperation had to work as long as their employers demanded for fear of losing their jobs?

**Worksheet 18 (**two pages) provides extension material on the religious beliefs of the Victorians to amplify the views expressed in Source 2.

# Section 6: How did people bring about change?

This new section covers the part of the Programme of Study which refers to the extension of the franchise, popular protest and reform.

This is done by a series of case studies: the abolition of slavery – a campaign involving a popular protest movement which is often ignored in textbooks; the story behind the passing of the 1832 Reform Act; a mainly urban popular protest movement (the Chartists) and a mainly rural one (the Rebecca Riots); the match workers' strike of 1888 and the beginnings of active working-class trade unions.

This section is then rounded off by a final 'survey' enquiry, which attempts to place these case studies in the context of nineteenth-century popular protest movements in general.

## ENQUIRY: WHY WAS SLAVERY ABOLISHED?

Pupils' Book pp.82–85

This two-spread enquiry is concerned mainly with the abolition of slavery, although the preceding abolition of the slave trade is also considered. The three main strands in this enquiry which need to be clearly brought out are as follows:
■ Different people had different, sometimes contradictory, motives for wishing to abolish slavery.
■ Abolition was not just the result of the work of white middle-class campaigners; the working classes, both black and white, played a vital role. It is important to emphasise that black people did not suffer slavery passively, and that their actions, both in Britain and in the Caribbean, were important in bringing about the end of slavery and the trade in slaves.
■ Slavery was not confined to the Empire, it was also practised in Britain.

The main part of the enquiry investigates the various factors at work in the fight against slavery. It would be possible to divide the class into groups, one group to consider each of the four factors. Each group could then

make a presentation to the rest of the class, highlighting the motives of the various campaigners. A class discussion could follow on the relative significance of these factors.

(Pages 82–83)

### Factor 1: The white middle-class campaigners
**Question 1:** Pupils might need some help with these cartoons. These are best discussed in class.

**Source 5:** Wilberforce's opponents spread rumours that he had a black mistress. Other objects in the cartoon suggest Wilberforce's duplicity, including the text 'Charity covereth a multitude of sins' in the book on the table, and a report of a perjury trial on the floor (only partly visible).

**Source 6:** The 'stirrer' is saying 'What! You cannot work because you are not well! I'll give you a warm bath.' The title will give pupils a hint of the artist's attitude; the small print at the bottom (not shown here) says that the story was corroborated by Fox and Wilberforce.

(Pages 84–85)

### Factor 4: Economics
**Summary question 3:** This is an important question, not only to balance out the material on page 75 but also to raise the deeper issue of how far racist attitudes can exist even where people are fighting for the rights of another racial group. This is an issue in anti-racist education today, as well, and is an important aspect of education for Citizenship.

## ENQUIRY: TRYING TO GET THE VOTE

Pupils' Book pp. 86–91
Worksheets 19, 20, 21

This three-spread enquiry covers the 1832 Reform Act – the background, the Act itself and the consequences of it.

It has enormous potential for teaching the cross-curricular theme of Citizenship, particularly in the first spread which compares the electoral system today with that in the 1820s; it is designed to create opportunities for analysing the democratic system of the 1820s, and also for discussing in class how British democracy works today.

(Pages 86–87)

### Democracy in the 1990s/Democracy in the 1820s
**Question 2:** One way of approaching this question would be to put each of the points in the 1820 list onto a separate card. Hand the cards out around the class for pupils to criticise. That way all the features will get some critical attention, instead of just the obvious ones.

**Source 3:** Pupils will probably need some help with

this cartoon, which could usefully be discussed in class. The same goes for the rest of the political cartoons in this enquiry: Sources 4, 7, 8, 11 and 16.

(Pages 88–89)

## Was reform needed?

By 1830 the arguments for and against reform had been going on for some time. If you are using this topic as your study in depth, you might wish to start your story further back in time with the earlier agitation for parliamentary reform which led to the Peterloo Massacre. One approach to investigating the Peterloo Massacre is to start with a newsroom simulation (**Worksheets 19 and 20**), leading into a detailed source evaluation exercise (**Worksheet 21**).

## The Peterloo Massacre – newsroom simulation

### Lesson 1: Preparation

Have the classroom laid out in groups of tables (five pupils to a table). All the resources for a newsroom simulation need to be on the tables (paper, glue, scissors, etc.) Explain what a newsroom simulation is and that the pupils will be doing one in full in the next lesson. They will need to work quickly while maintaining quality.

Go through **Worksheet 19** with the pupils to set the context. The rest of the lesson should be spent setting up the structure of the newspaper and outlining the task for lesson 2.

Before lesson 2 set up the information on **Worksheet 20** to be run through your computer or handed out manually.

### Lesson 2: The newsroom simulation

Lay out the room as in the previous lesson. The simulation should start as soon as possible. The 10 records (on **Worksheet 20**) should be printed out fairly quickly. If you don't have 'newsroom' software, simply photocopy and hand out the cards. A runner from each group collects each newsflash and takes it back to

his/her group. They discuss what seems to be happening and the types of article they might wish to produce for their paper. Give out a copy of the Cruikshank cartoon on **Worksheet 21** with the 1.35 record.

Once the tenth record has gone through at 2.15, pupils must start to make up their paper. Papers are to be finished by the end of the lesson.

### Lesson 3: Analysis. What really happened at St Peter's Fields?

Building on the newsroom simulation you can now look more closely at the evidence of what happened at St Peter's Fields. Evidence evaluation is quite difficult for pupils of this age, but they do already have some knowledge and hopefully some motivation for the topic. Explain how the 'Massacre' acquired the name 'Peterloo'.

Read through the sources on **Worksheet 21** with the pupils. Ensure they have an understanding of each one. Tackle questions 1–4 in class discussion. Pupils can then do question 5 as homework.

**Source 7:** 'Radical Reform' is about to ravish Britannia with a phallic spear; note also the sans-culotte liberty bonnet on his pike and the procession of murder, robbery, etc. in his wake.

**Source 8:** The tree contains the rotten boroughs – it is decaying and wormeaten, but propped up by the clergy. Is the King looking down from Constitution Hill in approval or disapproval?

**Question 1** is suitable for class discussion, particularly in classes where pupils may need some help with the cartoons.

**Activity:** The three viewpoints could also provide the basic material for a class debate on reform, in role or not.

(Pages 90–91)

## Why did the government agree to the reforms?

The timeline could be effectively presented on an OHP. Don't tell pupils the outcome of the arguments about

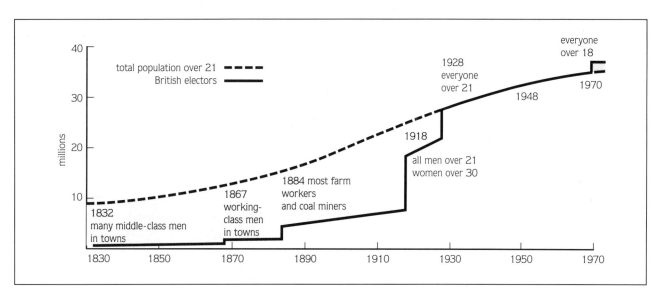

reform at first. Keep it as a question: would the government agree to reforms? Then tell the story of each stage – just in outline, as on the timeline – revealing one stage at a time. That way the passing of the Bill will appear more of a cliff-hanger than the timeline makes it appear.

**Question 1:** In Source 12A note the lecherous drunkenness of the rioters, their looting and attacks on property and the sedate and disciplined troops. In B note the defenceless rioters and merciless soldiers.

### Was the Reform Act great?

This may seem a somewhat provocative, or over-revisionist, interpretation of the Reform Act. But the material will encourage pupils to consider the immediate and long-term consequences of the Act.

### What happened later

**Summary question 1:** Go through the text and sources on page 91 with pupils, and discuss whether each provides evidence about immediate or long-term consequences. The diagram on page 39 shows the extension of the franchise after the 1832 Act.

### ENQUIRY: WERE THE CHARTISTS REVOLUTIONARIES?

Pupils' Book pp. 92–95
Worksheet 22

This two-spread enquiry continues our examination of parliamentary reform. As the first set of questions makes clear, the 1832 Reform Act did not deal with all the grievances of the working classes. The reform movement lived on.

The two main themes explored in this enquiry are:
■ the diversity of the Chartist movement. Many different types of people became Chartists. They also had many different reasons for supporting Chartism; the reasons covered here include the effects of the Poor Law, economic distress and unemployment, especially in the north, and jobs being destroyed by new machines. Finally, they had many different aims. It might appear that for some the political reforms they campaigned for were ends in themselves, while for others they were means to other, i.e. economic and social, ends
■ whether the Chartists were revolutionary.

(Pages 93–95)

### Were the Chartists violent? The case of Newport

**Source 16:** Pupils should interrogate these two pictures in detail before tackling the Activity. In A note the fleeing women and children, the crowds of protesters armed mainly with pikes, and the clouds of smoke around (coming from?) the hotel windows. In B note the Chartists firing on policemen armed only with truncheons.

**Worksheet 22** returns pupils to the key question of the enquiry: were the Chartists revolutionaries? If pupils have studied the unit on the French Revolution in Y8, it would be useful to recap a few of the methods and aims which characterised that revolution for comparison.

Different groups may come to different conclusions, which provides a good opportunity to discuss differing historical interpretations. There is plenty of scope for a variety of interpretations to emerge. Does O'Connor's Land Plan prove that the Chartists were reactionaries, looking back to a golden era in the past? Did the Chartists have conventional attitudes as regards the role of women? Were the Chartists a violent movement? Did the Chartists want merely to tinker with the system or to replace it completely?

### ENQUIRY: THE REBECCA RIOTS

Pupils' Book pp. 96–97
Worksheet 23

This single-spread enquiry on the Rebecca Riots provides a good contrast with the Chartists, one being urban in character, the other rural.

Pupils have already learned something about turnpike trusts in their work on transport, but here they are presented with a very different view of the turnpikes. The principal focus is on reasons for and results of the Rebecca Riots, but some of the questions do ask for a specific comparison with the Chartists.

### Trouble at the turnpikes

It might help pupils if they draw a timeline of the activities of Rebecca.

**Worksheet 23** is extension material on the treatment of the rioters by the authorities.

### ENQUIRY: WOMEN LEAD THE WAY

Pupils' Book pp. 98–99

This single-spread enquiry introduces pupils to yet another form of nineteenth-century organisation and protest: trade unions and strikes. The match workers' strike has been chosen because it represented something of a watershed for working-class unions. It paved the way for other previously powerless workers to mount battles for better pay or conditions – most notably the dockers, who staged a successful strike the following year.

**Source 1:** Health and safety at work are taken for granted as an important priority today, but not so in the 1880s.

Pupils might consider how successful the reforms investigated on pages 80–81 had been if conditions such as these still existed as late as 1888.

## ENQUIRY: POPULAR PROTEST MOVEMENTS

Pupils' Book pp. 100–101

This single-spread enquiry has been designed as a 'survey' enquiry to help put the earlier case studies into some context. It will give pupils an overall idea of the major trends in popular protest movements.

By using the timeline, pupils will also be able to decide for themselves whether there was any continuous development in the methods and aims of the protesters, or whether it is impossible to detect a pattern.

This could lead to an examination of the methods of popular protest used today, and a discussion of which methods are legitimate and which can never be justified – an important idea in the theme of Citizenship.

**Source 4:** Pupils should interrogate this in detail. It shows different types of ships: (clockwise from centre left) line of battle ship, armour clad turret ship, Atlantic liner *British Empire*, barque and yacht, tug and yawl, and a lifeboat. Note also the detailed construction scene. At the bottom are pictures representing the benefits paid: (anticlockwise from top left) unemployment, compensation, accident, pensions, sickness and widows' pensions.

**Question 1:** You could make a grid for pupils to use.

**Question 4:** Pupils may need some help with this. Get them to think about how desperate the protesters were, how organised their movement was, and whether there was any real alternative to violence.

# Section 7: Conclusion

## ENQUIRY: THE TWO FACES OF LONDON

Pupils' Book pp. 102–105
Worksheets 24, 25

What was Britain like in 1900? This two-spread enquiry gives two pictures – or rather two sides of the same coin. On the one hand, pupils are presented with all that was impressive about London by the end of the nineteenth century, but turn the page and they are confronted by another side of life in London.

(Pages 102–103)

### The imperial capital
#### Question 1:
■ guano = the long-accumulated excrement of certain sea birds, found on some coasts and islands, especially around South America. It was, and still is, used for manure.

■ alizarin = a red dye extracted from the roots of the plant madder, but now mostly prepared chemically.

■ gutta percha = a whitish rubber substance, made from the latex of certain tropical plants, used in electrical insulation, waterproofing and dentistry.

**Activity:** Pupils can use DTP to design and present their leaflets.

(Pages 104–105)

### Living in the East End
The written evidence used here is entirely genuine: it has been taken from Charles Booth's report, and the places and families mentioned are historical. The drawing of Shelton Street is a reconstruction based on Booth's descriptions. It might be worth pointing out to pupils that this is an artist's cutaway, rather than a house whose wall has collapsed!

**Questions 1 and 2:** The pupils will need **Worksheets 24 and 25** to complete these questions. They will need two copies of Worksheet 24 to fill in all the people mentioned.

## ENQUIRY: IMAGES OF THE VICTORIANS

Pupils' Book pp. 106–107
Worksheets 1, 26

This single-spread enquiry concludes the unit and provides teachers with a final opportunity to look at historical interpretations.

### How the Victorians saw themselves
**Source 2:** We don't know the identity of all the figures, but the faces we can identify are: Charles Darwin (top left), Isambard Kingdom Brunel (centre right), Joseph Lister, who pioneered the use of antiseptics in surgery (bottom right), Rowland Hill, who set up the 'penny post' in 1840 (bottom centre), Thomas Huxley, a great biologist (bottom left), Michael Faraday, a pioneer of electricity (centre left) and Herbert Spencer, a philosopher (under Darwin).

### How other people have seen the Victorians
**Source 10:** The poster (in fact the jacket of the video) is a poor substitute for showing the film if you have access to it. Choose two contrasting extracts – for example one showing middle-class life (*Who Will Buy?*) and one showing working-class life (*Consider Yourself One of Us*).

**Sources 7–11** could be used to introduce a more general discussion about the different ways in which the past is used.

■ Pupils would probably be able to suggest other examples of images of the past being used in advertisements.

■ They might also be able to suggest other purposes for which the past is used, e.g. to support one's own political views (see page 64), to justify one's own career (you only have to look at the spate of political memoirs published recently), to support or to attack the status quo (it wasn't like this in my day) and so on.

An opportunity for investigating historical interpretations is provided by **Worksheet 26** (two pages). This takes a completely different approach and considers the ways in which the Victorians themselves viewed and used the past. The sources and the questions are challenging, and the worksheet should be used as an extension exercise for more able pupils.

This would also be a good opportunity to return to **Worksheet 1** to review all the changes which happened over the period 1750–1900 in the light of all the information gained during the study of the unit.

# Britain 1750–1900: what changed?

YOU have been asked to design additional panels for the first six pages of your textbook (see pages 2–7). The possible topics for the extra panels are:

Work in groups.
1. Choose three topics which you think are the most important.
2. Find some pictures to illustrate your chosen topics for 1750, 1825 and 1900. You will find some pictures you could use in your textbook, but you will also need to do some research in the school library.
3. Write captions to go with your pictures.
4. Mount your chosen material onto a display.

## The British Empire

## Religion

## Life in towns

## Life in the countryside

## Styles of architecture

## Pollution and the environment

Now, working on your own, write the answers to these questions in your exercise book to explain what you have put in your display.
5. Explain why you think the three topics you chose were important in the period 1750–1900.
6. For each topic, explain how much change occurred between 1750 and 1900.
7. Explain whether these changes benefited most people, or harmed most people, or had little effect on them.

# Growth factors

1. Fill in this grid for the businessmen you have studied. Write brief notes on the grid showing how each factor was at work in the growth of each business.

2. Use the information in your grid to write an essay entitled

'What made businesses grow in the eighteenth and nineteenth centuries?' In your essay use examples from the businesses you have studied. You can either concentrate on just one business or try to use examples from several of them.

| | Name: | Name: | Name: | Name: | Name: |
|---|---|---|---|---|---|
| **Factor 1:**<br>**the market grows** | | | | | |
| **Factor 2:**<br>**production grows** | | | | | |
| **Factor 3:**<br>**investment grows** | | | | | |

# Why do businesses grow?

SOURCES 1– 6 show six steps a businessman or woman might take to help a business to grow.

1. Match Sources 1– 6 to the following captions:
   - Cut prices
   - Improve transport
   - Advertise products
   - Borrow more money
   - Train workers better
   - Buy new and better machinery
2. Explain why each action might help a business to grow.
3. In the stories of the businessmen you have studied, find one example of each action being taken.

**SOURCE 1**

**SOURCE 2**

**SOURCE 3**

**SOURCE 4**

**SOURCE 5**

**SOURCE 6**

# Richard Arkwright

The captions on the right describe important events in the story of Richard Arkwright. Some are things he did. Some are things other people did which helped him.

**1.** Using pages 12–13 of your textbook, find out when each event took place. Then draw a line from the caption to the correct date on your timeline.

**2.** Choose three captions and say how each one helped Arkwright to be successful.

---

*The flying shuttle makes weaving much faster than spinning*

*James Hargreaves invents a spinning jenny, but it is a very complicated machine*

*Arkwright invents his own spinning machine*

*Arkwright's business partners buy him a patent on his spinning machine*

*Arkwright builds his first factory*

*Arkwright builds his first water-powered factory*

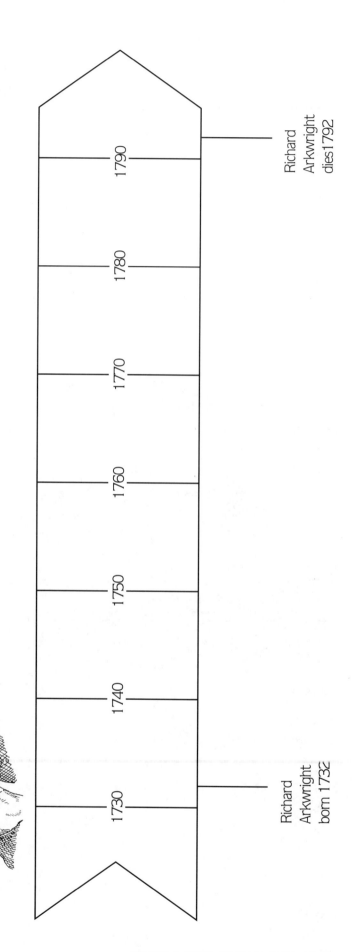

1730

Richard Arkwright born 1732

1740

1750

1760

1770

1780

1790

Richard Arkwright dies 1792

# A new view of society

**SOURCE 1** From Robert Owen, *A New View of Society*, 1813

*If ... due care as to the state of your inanimate machines can produce ... beneficial results, what may not be expected if you devote equal attention to your vital machines [workers], which are far more wonderfully constructed? ... You will discover that the latter may be easily trained and directed to procure a large increase of pecuniary gain [to make bigger profits] ...*

**SOURCE 2** From Robert Owen, *A New View of Society*, 1813

*Train any population rationally, and they will be rational.*

**SOURCE 3** From Robert Owen, *Observations upon the Effect of the Manufacturing System*, 1815

*The general diffusion [spread] of manufactures throughout a country generates a new character in its inhabitants ... The acquisition of wealth, and the desire which it naturally creates for a continued increase, have introduced a fondness for ... luxuries ... and they have also generated a disposition ... to sacrifice the best feelings of human nature to this love of accumulation ... The industry of the lower orders, from whose labour this wealth is now drawn, has been carried by new competitors striving against those of longer standing, to a point of real oppression, reducing them ... to a state ... infinitely more degraded and miserable than they were before the introduction of these manufactories, upon the success of which their bare subsistence now depends.*

**SOURCE 4** From Robert Owen, *Report to the County of Lanark*, 1821

*The principle of individual interest, opposed as it is perpetually to the public good, is considered, by the most celebrated political economists, to be the corner-stone to the social system, and without which, society could not subsist.*

*Yet when they shall know themselves, and discover the wonderful effects which combination and union can produce, they will acknowledge that the present arrangement of society is the most anti-social, impolitic, and irrational that can be devised ...*

**SOURCE 5** From a letter by a nineteenth-century economist, David Ricardo

*Can any reasonable person believe, with Owen, that a society, such as he projects, will flourish and produce more than has ever yet been produced by an equal number of men, if they are to be stimulated to exertion by a regard to the community, instead of by a regard to their private interest? Is not the experience of ages against him?*

**3.** Whom do you agree with more, Owen (Sources 1–4) or Ricardo (Source 5)?

**1.** What change in Owen's thinking can you see between Source 1 and Source 3?
**2.** What was it that Owen most disliked about the kind of society that was being produced by the growth of industry?

# Arkwright or Owen?

ARKWRIGHT and Owen were both important businessmen. But was one more important than the other? This is a more complicated question than it seems. One of them may have been important during his lifetime, while the other may have had a greater influence on people since. Even looking at their importance while they were alive is not straightforward, because they may have been important in completely different ways.

The following chart will help you to organise your thoughts about the importance of these two businessmen.

|  | Arkwright | Owen |
|---|---|---|
| What did he invent? |  |  |
| How successful was he as a businessman during his lifetime? |  |  |
| How much did he contribute to the development of new industries? |  |  |
| How much did he influence people's attitudes about how workers should be treated and how businesses should be run? |  |  |
| How much influence has he had on people's attitudes since his lifetime? |  |  |

# Would you have made a good entrepreneur?

YOU have read about a number of successful businessmen. How successful would you have been as an entrepreneur in the eighteenth and nineteenth centuries?

Look at the following problems, which businessmen faced during this period. Decide which course of action you would have taken in each case. You must give a reason for your choice.

Your teacher will then help you add up your score and you can see how well you'd have succeeded as a businessman or woman.

**1.** Your business has at last made a profit. Do you

a) spend the money on a new house for your family *or* ☐
b) invest the money in the business to buy the latest machinery *or* ☐
c) leave the money in the bank to earn interest? ☐

**2.** You have just invented a new spinning machine. Do you:

a) keep the invention a secret *or* ☐

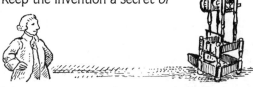

b) boast to everyone about your invention and let them borrow it *or* ☐
c) take out a patent on the invention? ☐

**3.** You own a textile factory. You need more workers. Do you:

a) employ the cheapest workers you can find, and save money by paying them very little and spending nothing on their welfare *or* ☐
b) employ the fittest and strongest workers you can find, then work them as hard as you can until they drop from exhaustion *or* ☐
c) employ the fittest workers you can find and look after them: educate their children, build decent housing for them? ☐

**4.** You own a pottery business. You sell all your products locally. Do you:

a) carry on as you are *or* ☐
b) advertise your products all over the country *or* ☐
c) carry out research to see what new products are needed to widen your markets? ☐

**5.** You run an iron works. You are being charged more and more for your raw materials – coal, iron ore and limestone – by the local mine and quarry owners. Do you:

a) try to find a new source of raw materials from further afield *or* ☐
b) buy up the local mines and quarries *or* ☐

c) charge your customers more for your iron? ☐

**6.** There's a great demand for bricks to build houses in the growing new towns. You run a successful brick works. Do you:

a) save up the profits until you have enough money in a few years' time to extend your brick works *or* ☐
b) bring in a partner with money to extend your brick works now *or* ☐
c) sell off your business to a rival while things are going well? ☐

**Your score**
**15–18:** You are a brilliant entrepreneur.
**10–15:** You make some good decisions, but you are a bit too cautious.
**6–9:** You've got a lot to learn about business!

# The changing face of farming

**Problem**
Crops had changed very little since the Middle Ages.

**Problem**
Farmers did not think about growing food to sell. They just grew enough to feed themselves.

**Problem**
A lot of land was needed for animals to graze.

**Problem**
One of the three open fields was left fallow (empty) every year.

**Problem**
Farming tasks were mainly done by hand, as they had been in the Middle Ages.

**Problem**
The long thin strips in the open fields made it difficult to use machinery.

**Problem**
The farmers were too poor to invest in new machinery.

**Problem**
It was difficult to experiment with new ideas, because everyone in the village had to agree about changes to the use of the open fields.

**Problem**
Some soil was not good enough to grow crops.

**Change**
New crops were grown for animals to eat.

**Change**
Animals were carefully bred and fed, and grew larger.

**Change**
New crop rotations were tried out. New crops put goodness back into the soil, so there was no need to leave a field fallow (empty) every third year.

**Change**
New machines were invented to speed up tasks that had been done by hand.

**Change**
When fields were enclosed they were reorganised into more efficient shapes, where machinery was easier to use.

**Change**
The price of food went up as the size of the population grew. Farmers who sold food found they could get a lot of money for it.

**Change**
Individual farmers could try out new ideas on their own enclosed land.

**Change**
Information about changes was spread by writers and societies.

**Change**
New, stronger farm tools were developed, such as ploughs made of iron.

**Change**
Fertilisers were tried out to improve the quality of the soil.

# Shrinking Britain

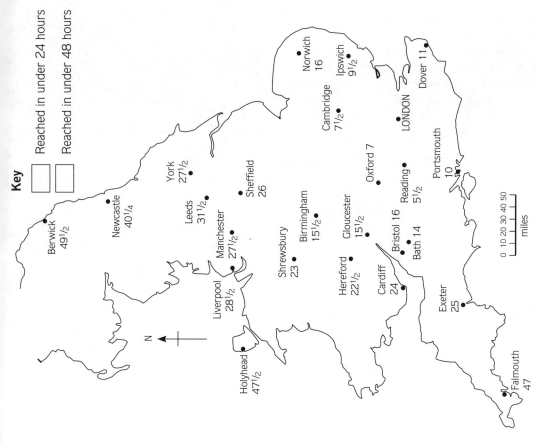

**Key**

☐ Reached in under 24 hours

☐ Reached in under 48 hours

Berwick 49½

Newcastle 40¼

York 27½

Sheffield 26

Leeds 31½

Manchester 27½

Liverpool 28½

Holyhead 47½

Shrewsbury 23

Birmingham 15½

Hereford 22½

Gloucester 15½

Cardiff 24

Bristol 16

Bath 14

Exeter 25

Falmouth 47

Norwich 16

Ipswich 9½

Cambridge 7½

Oxford 7

Reading 5½

LONDON

Dover 11

Portsmouth 10

N

0 10 20 30 40 50
miles

**SOURCE 2** Journey times to the same places in 1811

4. Use the same colours to show the situation in 1811. Don't forget to fill in the key as well.

5. Write a paragraph explaining the changes the maps show.

**Key**

☐ Reached in under 24 hours

☐ Reached in under 48 hours

Edinburgh 230

Newcastle 132

York 84

Sheffield 60

Leeds 84

Manchester 80

Liverpool 84

Shrewsbury 75

Birmingham 36

Banbury 30

Hereford 63

Gloucester 39

Cirencester 22

Bristol 40

Bath 36

Trowbridge 24

Exeter 40

Oxford 13

Abingdon 14

Newbury 12

Norwich 36

Ipswich 24

Cambridge 24

LONDON

Dover 27

Brighton 14

N

0 10 20 30 40 50
miles

**SOURCE 1** Journey times from London for a stage coach in 1750

1. In one colour shade in the area of Source 1 that can be reached from London by stage coach in less than 24 hours.

2. In another colour shade the area that can be reached from London in less than 48 hours.

3. Fill in the key using your chosen colours.

# Planning the Liverpool and Manchester Railway

As an industrialist who has to move goods between Liverpool and Manchester, you have been asked to take part in a survey by the Provisional Committee. Fill in the questionnaire below to give the committee the information it requires in assessing the region's transport needs.

*Provisional Committee
of Liverpool and Manchester
Industrialists*

Name: _____

Please give some details of your business, e.g. what type of goods you have to move:

_____

_____

_____

Which route do you use at present?

_____

_____

Why do you use this route?

_____

_____

_____

Please give details of any problems you encounter in transporting your goods this way:

_____

_____

_____

_____

_____

# Was the railway a success?

## What people hoped would happen

**SOURCE 1** From the *Quarterly Review*, 1825

*"By the establishment of a railway, the inhabitants of Liverpool will be entitled to buy their coals several shillings per ton cheaper. By opening the collieries to the sea, Liverpool will become one of the greatest shipping ports for coal. A railway will help the conveyance of agricultural produce, and iron and limestone throughout the manufacturing districts of Lancashire. Nor are the advantages merely local. The journey from Manchester to Dublin will be reduced to eighteen or twenty hours, and the price of Irish corn, flax, linen and butter in Lancashire will be considerably reduced."*

A merchant in Liverpool selling cotton

A canal owner

## What did happen

**SOURCE 2** From the annual register in 1832, two years after the railway opened

*"All the coaches have stopped running. The canals have reduced their prices by 30 per cent. Goods are delivered in Manchester the same day as they arrive in Liverpool. By canal it took three days. The saving to manufacturers in Manchester, in the transporting of cotton alone, has been £20,000 a year. Coal pits have been sunk and factories established along the railway, giving greater employment to the poor. The railway pays one fifth of the poor rates in the parishes through which it passes. The transportation of milk and garden produce is easier. Residents along the line can use the railways to attend their business in Manchester and Liverpool with ease and little expense. No inconvenience is felt by residents from smoke or noise. The value of land on the line has gone up because of the railway. It is much sought after for building."*

A Manchester cotton mill owner

An unemployed person in Liverpool

1. Explain whether each of the people shown could benefit from the Liverpool and Manchester Railway. Fill in the speech bubbles to show how each one might feel about it.

A farmer on the railway route

# The quality of life

HERE is a list of questions that we might ask someone to measure their quality of life.

## Jobs
- Is their job boring or interesting?
- Is it hard or easy?
- Is it dangerous or safe?
- Is getting a job easy?
- Is their job secure?

## Pay and prices
- How much are they paid?
- Are they paid more or less than other people?
- Can they earn extra income from doing other jobs?
- How much do basics (food, heating, etc.) cost?
- How much of their pay goes on these basics?
- How much do luxury goods cost?

## Health
- Are they healthy?
- How long can they expect to live?
- Is the environment clean and healthy?
- If they are ill, are they able to see a doctor?

## Home life
- Do members of their family live together?
- Is their house large enough and comfortable?
- Do they have any leisure time?
- What can they afford to do in their leisure time?
- Do they receive any education?

---

1. What ideas did you have on your list which are not here?
2. Underline four questions which you think are the most important of all. Explain your choice.

---

Now look at the following points. Most historians would agree about these descriptions of changes between 1750 and 1900.

- Upper- and middle-class people were generally wealthier in 1900 than they were in 1750.

- By 1900 the overall standard of living was higher than it had been in 1850.

- Between 1750 and 1850 some working-class people became better off, while others became worse off. Those who were better off tended to be living in the new industrial areas. But the wages of some people in industrial areas fell, such as the handloom weavers after the invention of the power loom.

- Developments in industry and transport made many goods much cheaper.

- Many more people worked in factories. This affected their freedom to organise their own working life.

- During the nineteenth century life for industrial workers improved because of new laws and the development of trade unions.

- Living conditions in the new industrial towns were generally bad until the mid-nineteenth century, but then they improved.

- Educational opportunities for most of the population increased between 1750 and 1900.

- There is not enough evidence to reach firm conclusions on many of the questions.

---

3. Look again at the four categories we started with: jobs, pay and prices, health and home life. From the information above, did life get better for most people in all these categories?

---

# The Glovers and the Eyles

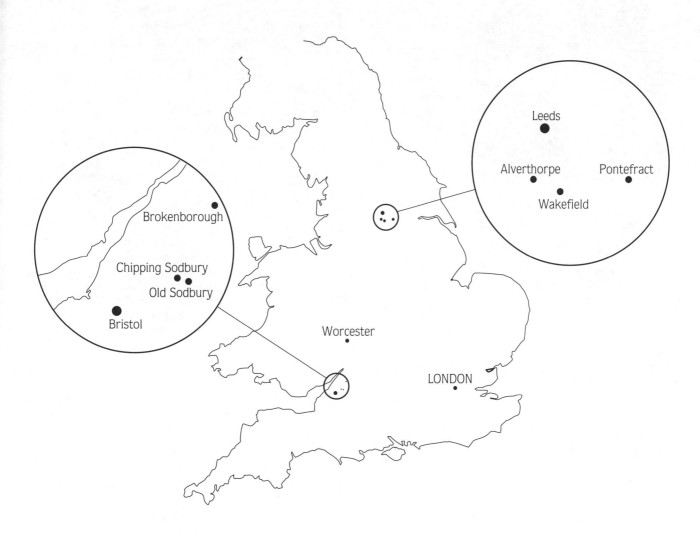

## SOURCE 1

On Source 1, show the movements of the different generations of the Glover and Eyles families. Follow these instructions.

■ **Stage 1:** rough planning. Make a list of all the people, then beside their names write down where they lived and any moves they made.
■ **Stage 2:** you are now ready to transfer this information onto the map. Use a different colour for each generation. Make sure it is clear which family is which.

■ **Stage 3:** conclusions. Did the later generations of the two families move around more than the earliest generation? Did the Glovers or the Eyles move more?
■ **Stage 4:** comparisons. If you have been researching your own family history, draw the movements of your parents and grandparents onto the map in a different colour. You may need a map showing a much larger area. Has your family moved more or less than the Glovers and the Eyles?

# Charlotte Guest

**SOURCE 1**
A painting of Lady Charlotte Guest

MOST of the people who ran businesses in the eighteenth and nineteenth centuries were men. But there were a few exceptions, women who made a success of what was looked upon as a man's job.

Lady Charlotte Bertie married Josiah John Guest, owner of the Dowlais iron works, in 1833. For a member of the nobility to marry an industrialist – even a very wealthy one like Guest – was regarded as a step down the social ladder. But Lady Charlotte was very proud of the Dowlais works, which at that time was said to be the largest of its kind in the world. She took a great interest in the iron and coal industries and the people who worked in them. She learned Welsh (the language spoken by most of the Dowlais workers at that time).

Charlotte Guest visited the works frequently, went down the coal mines and helped her husband with the accounts and letter writing. When he became ill and then died (in 1852), she took over the management of the works herself. This was a very unusual position for a woman in the mid-nineteenth century.

She took a particular interest in the education of the workers' children. The Dowlais schools employed trained teachers and used methods similar to those at New Lanark. In 1851, new school buildings designed by Sir Charles Barry (the architect of the Houses of Parliament) were built. Lady Charlotte also helped to organise a night school for the adult workers, a library, and a savings bank. Despite all of these improvements, however, the living conditions of most of the workers remained very poor.

Sources 2–5 are adapted from Lady Charlotte's journals from the 1850s.

**SOURCE 2**
"I have given myself a man's education from the age of twelve . . . and since I married, I have taken up such pursuits as . . . would make me familiar with what occupied the male part of the population."

**SOURCE 3**
"Whatever I do, I must do better than anyone else. I cannot endure anything in a second grade. I am happy to see we are at the head of the iron trade. Otherwise, I could not take pride in my house in the City and my Works at Dowlais and glory (playfully) in being (in some sort) a tradeswoman."

**SOURCE 4** Charlotte Guest describes a visit to Mr Lucy, a businessman in Bristol, to discuss the supply of rails to the Midland Counties Railway

"[Mr Lucy] seemed at first rather surprised at seeing me, but we soon began discussing questions of freight, interest, etc., as comfortably as if I had not the shame of being of weaker sex and intellect than himself."

**SOURCE 5** Charlotte Guest describes her feelings towards the workforce on returning to Dowlais after a new lease of the works had been agreed

"May we indeed be able to do them good, and under a reviving trade have it in our power to minister to the necessities, etc., not only bodily but to their improvements in every respect, in some measure to justify the warmth of their reception towards us. It is a heavy responsibility."

1. What evidence do Sources 2–5 provide that Lady Charlotte's position at Dowlais was regarded as unusual?
2. Suggest why
a) it was difficult for women to be industrialists and factory owners in the nineteenth century
b) Lady Charlotte was able to occupy such a position.
3. What was Lady Charlotte's attitude towards the people of Merthyr Tydfil? Was it in any way a typical Victorian attitude?

# Skilled or unskilled?

---

> **1.** Look at this list of jobs. Decide which of them would be skilled jobs and which would be unskilled.

■ Unloading the coal, iron ore and limestone.

■ Making coal into coke in the coke ovens.

■ Breaking up the blocks of limestone into smaller pieces suitable for the blast furnace.

■ Filling up the blast furnaces. N.B. Blast furnaces were loaded from the top.

■ Tapping the blast furnace: this involved opening holes at the bottom of the blast furnace at exactly the right moment to allow the molten iron to flow out.

■ Taking away the waste from the blast furnaces.

■ Puddling: puddlers had to stir the molten iron in the puddling furnace, and then, at just the right moment as it formed a spongy mass, lift it out with a long pair of tongs.

■ Moving the iron between the blast furnaces, the puddling furnaces, the forge hammers and the rollers.

# Brighton

━━━━━━━━━━━━━━━━━━━━━━━━━━━━━━━━━━━━ *continued* ▶

**1.** Compare Sources 1 and 2. List five important changes that took place between 1779 and 1824.

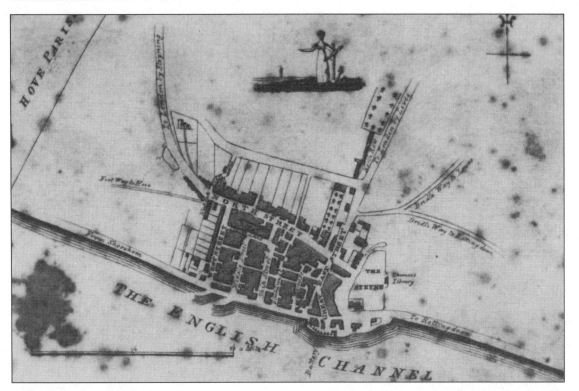

**SOURCE 1** Brighton in 1779

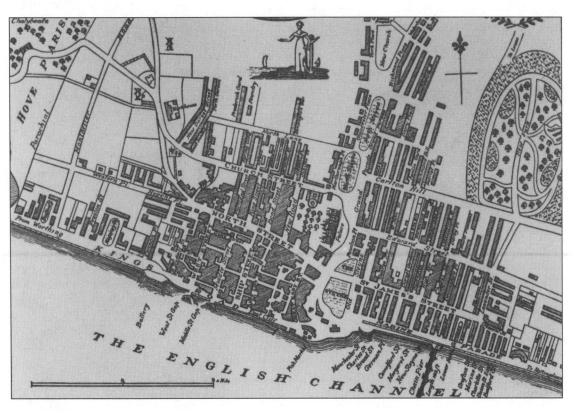

**SOURCE 2** Brighton in 1824

*continued* ▶

*continued* ▶

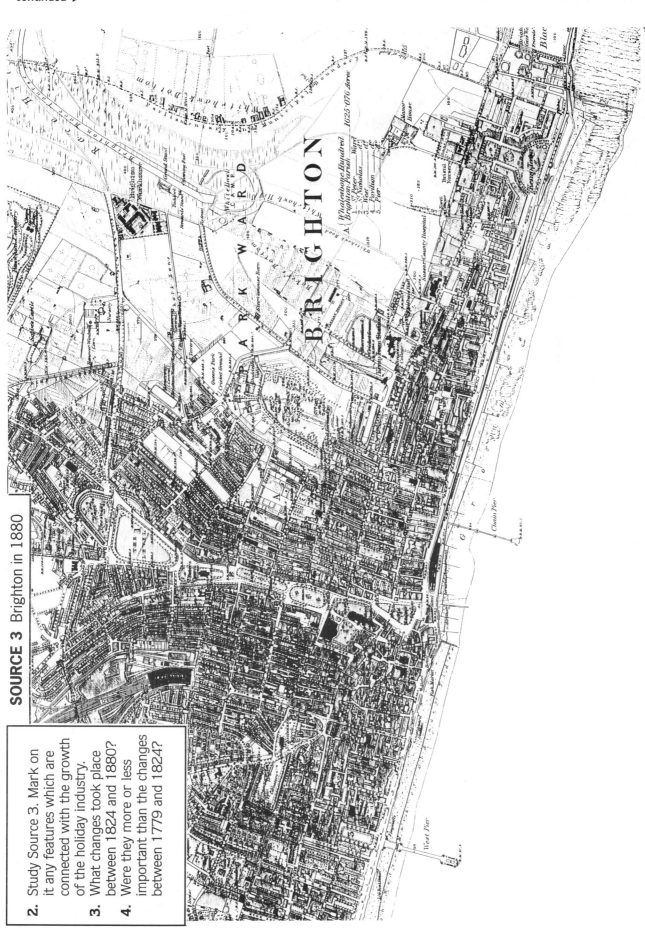

**SOURCE 3** Brighton in 1880

2. Study Source 3. Mark on it any features which are connected with the growth of the holiday industry.

3. What changes took place between 1824 and 1880?

4. Were they more or less important than the changes between 1779 and 1824?

# Work

**SOURCE 1** Extracts from Ford Madox Brown's own comments on his painting *Work*, 1863

" *This picture was begun in 1852 at Hampstead. At that time extensive excavations, connected with the supply of water, were going on in the neighbourhood, and seeing and studying daily as I did the British navvy in the full swing of his activity, it appeared to me that he was at least as worthy of the powers of an English painter as the peasant of the Campagna [in Italy]. Gradually this idea developed itself into that of* Work *as it now exists, with the British navvy for the central group as the outward and visible type of 'Work'.*

■ *Here are represented the young navvy in the pride of manly health and beauty; the strong fully developed navvy who does his work and loves his beer; the selfish old stout bachelor navvy; the navvy of strong animal nature; and Paddy with his pipe in his mouth.*

*The young navvy who occupies the place of hero in the picture stands on a platform placed half-way down the trench; two men from beneath shovel the earth up to him, and he shovels it on to the pile outside.*

■ *Next in significance is the ragged wretch who has never been taught to work, with his restless gleaming eyes. He lives in Flower and Dean Street, where the policemen walk two and two. Before dawn you may see him miles out in the country, collecting his wild weeds and plants.*

■ *In the opposite corner of the picture are two men who appear to have nothing to do. These are the brainworkers, who are seemingly idle.*

■ *Next to these, on the shaded bank, are different characters out of work: haymakers in quest of employment; an Irishman with hay stuffed in his hat to keep the draught out; a young shoeless Irishman, with his wife, feeding their first-born with cold pap; an old sailor turned haymaker; and two young peasants in search of harvest work reduced in strength by lack of food.*

■ *Behind the ragged wretch, appears a very different group who, from an opposite cause, have perhaps not been sufficiently used to work either. These are the rich, who have no need to work. The pastry-cook's tray, symbol of superfluity, accompanies these. Past the pastry-cook come two married ladies. The elder of the two has just flung a tract entitled* The Hodman's Haven or drink for thirsty souls *to one of the navvies, who scorns it. This well-intentioned lady has perhaps never reflected that navvies may have notions to the effect that ladies might be benefited by receiving tracts containing navvies' ideas – as navvies are skilled workmen and men of great experience.*

■ *In front of her is the lady whose only business in life as yet is to dress and look beautiful for our benefit. She probably possesses everything that can give enjoyment to life. Would anyone wish it otherwise? Certainly not I, dear lady. Only in your own interest, seeing that certain blessings like health and beauty cannot be insured for ever, I would beg to call your attention to the small, exceedingly ragged, dirty children in the foreground.*

■ *They are motherless. As to the father, I have no doubt he drinks and neglects them. The eldest girl, not more than ten, is very worn looking and thin, her frock the gift of some grown-up person. However, the younger ones are taken care of, and nestle to her as to a mother. The sunburnt baby looks well fed and has even been put into mourning for mother. The other little, though it sucks a piece of carrot in place of a sugar-plum, and is shoeless, seems healthy and happy. The care of the two little ones is an anxious charge for the elder girl, and she has become a premature scold through having to manage that boy who is the plague of her life, as boys always are.*

■ *The couple on horseback in the middle distance consists of a rich gentleman and his daughter. There is also a man with a beer tray. On the wall are posters; one of the Boy's Home, 41 Euston Road, which the lady giving out tracts will no doubt place the urchin playing with the barrow in. Back in the distance we see an Assembly Room where Professor Snoox is about to repeat his interesting lecture on the habits of the domestic cat. Indignant pusses up on the roofs are denying his theory in toto.*

■ *In the background a policeman has caught an orange-girl in the heinous offence of resting her basket on a post, and who himself administers justice in the shape of a push, that sends her fruit all over the road.* "

---

1. Look again at your answers to questions 1–3 on page 65 of your textbook. Now that you have read the artist's notes on his own painting, how would you change your answers?

# How religious were the Victorians?

RELIGION played a larger part in most people's lives in eighteenth- and nineteenth-century Britain than it does today.

In 1750 the biggest religious group was the Church of England. The Church of England rector or vicar was a central figure in most communities, especially rural ones. However, some people felt that the Church of England was getting out of touch with the poor, especially in the areas where the new industries were developing.

One of these people was John Wesley, who travelled around the country from 1738 until his death in 1790, preaching directly to ordinary people. He gained many supporters, who became known as 'Methodists'. They broke away from the Church of England in 1784.

In 1811 the Methodists split into two groups. One group were called the Primitive Methodists. This group particularly attracted unskilled workers, such as agricultural labourers (Ashill had a Primitive Methodist chapel) and miners. The other group were known as the Wesleyan Methodists. They gained much of their support from skilled workers, craftsmen and shopkeepers. All Methodists stressed the importance of hard work, 'temperance' (avoiding alcohol) and charity. Their chapels were built in towns and villages all over the country.

There were also other groups outside the Church of England, such as Unitarians and Congregationalists, whose members were mainly middle-class or lower middle-class. Together, all these groups became known as 'Non-conformists'. In some parts of the country, for example Wales, there were more Non-conformists than Anglicans (members of the Church of England).

There were also changes happening within the Church of England itself. There were people who, like the Methodists, wanted to reach out to poorer people in the towns. They became involved in 'humanitarian' campaigns, such as the struggle against slavery and the factory reform movement. This was known as the 'evangelical revival'. Evangelicals worked to get new churches built in the industrial towns, and tried to make better-off people aware of the conditions in which the poor were living.

There were many Roman Catholics in the towns, too, especially in communities of Irish immigrants.

A final group which involved itself in work with the poor was the Salvation Army, founded in 1880 by a Methodist, William Booth. The Salvation Army saw itself as a missionary force and was organised like a real army, with uniforms and bands.

Despite the work of all the religious groups, there were many influences around to turn people away from religion. The churches found it very difficult to cope with the new social situation in the towns. New scientific discoveries, and especially the theory of evolution set out by Charles Darwin in his book, *The Origin of Species*, in 1859, made many educated people reconsider their beliefs.

In 1851 a religious census measured for the first time how many people actually went to church. It showed that fewer people went to church in the towns than anyone had really expected. Attendance at religious services actually decreased in the second half of the nineteenth century.

SOURCE 1 A photograph of an evangelical bible stall in Oxford, 1880

*continued* ▶

► continued

**SOURCE 2** St Anne's Church in Highgate, London, built in 1853

**SOURCE 4**
A photograph of a Methodist chapel in Wales built in 1878

**SOURCE 3** From *The Bitter Cry of Outcast London*, by Andrew Mearns, 1883

"*Whilst we have been building our churches and solacing ourselves with our religion . . . the poor have been growing poorer, the wretched more miserable, and the immoral more corrupt; the gulf has been daily widening which separates the lowest classes of the community from our churches and chapels, and from all decency and civilisation . . .*

*. . . We find in the neighbourhood of Old Ford, in 147 consecutive houses, inhabited for the most part by the respectable working class, 212 families, 118 of which never, under any circumstances, attend a place of worship. Out of 2290 persons living in consecutive houses at Bow Common, only 88 adults and 47 children ever attend, and as 64 of these are connected with one Mission Hall, only 24 out of the entire number worship elsewhere. One street off Leicester Square contains 246 families, and only twelve of these are ever represented at the house of God.*"

1. Make a list of all the religious groups mentioned on these two pages. Alongside the name of each group, put all the information you can find about who supported it and where it was strong.
2. Why might more people go to church in the countryside than in the towns?
3. How religious do you think the Victorians were? Support your answer with evidence from these two pages.

# The Peterloo Massacre of 1819

AFTER the war against France ended in 1815, there was a period of unrest in Britain. Jobs were hard to find, wages were low, and rent and prices were high. Many people amongst the middle and working classes thought the only way to improve things was to change the way the country was being governed. They believed that 'good' laws would only be introduced if *more* people had the vote. Remember that only 2.7% of the population could vote at this time.

A group of people calling themselves Radicals began to hold mass meetings and marches to win support for their ideas. Henry Hunt and William Cobbett were two of the most important leaders. The government was concerned about their activities and kept a close eye on them. The Radicals called a meeting at St Peter's Fields near Manchester on 16 August 1819.

---

**1.** Look at the map below. Suggest why Manchester would be a good place for the Radicals to hold a meeting.

---

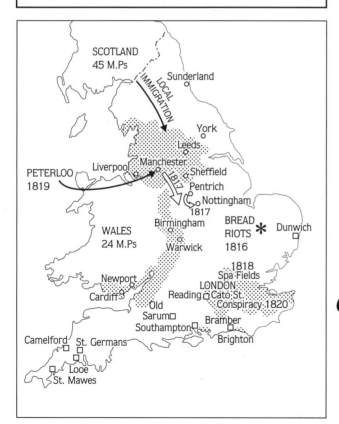

Legend:
- □ Notorious rotten borough
- ▒ Population increasing but not representational
- ○ Industrial town
- ⌇ Uprising 1817

## Preparation for the meeting at St Peter's Fields

The meeting at St Peter's Fields was expected to be *big*. It was estimated that between 50,000 and 80,000 people would turn up (about the number which can fit into Wembley Stadium today). There is evidence that both the authorities and the people going to the meeting had made some preparations.

### The local magistrates

Magistrates are responsible for *law and order*. The magistrates in Manchester were worried about the meeting at St Peter's Fields. Most were quite well off and didn't want the ordinary working men to have a say in government. There had recently been a revolution in France and that had led to a great deal of violence. The magistrates thought there might be violence at this meeting and therefore decided to call in the King's Hussars (cavalry) and make ready the Yeomanry (reserve cavalry). The Yeomanry were men who were in respectable jobs but were called up when needed. They had no love for the Radicals, and would not be as disciplined as the professional soldiers.

### The demonstrators

Opinion seems to have differed as to whether the demonstrators were looking for trouble. One eye witness commented:

> " *I saw the march proceeding towards St Peter's Fields, and never saw a happier sight. The so-called "marching order" was like children going to Sunday School. We laughed at the fears of the magistrates, and the remark was made that if the men intended mischief they would not have brought their wives and children with them.* "

However, the *Courier* newspaper said:

> " *Before 12 o'clock crowds began to assemble, each village having a banner, and some a cap with "Liberty" painted on it. Each part kept in military order with sticks to their soldiers.* "

# The newsroom

**12.00**
Crowds are beginning to assemble at St Peter's Fields near Manchester. You can see which towns and villages people come from by the banners they carry. Some have banners saying 'Votes for all', others have caps with 'Liberty' written on them. One banner says 'Die like men, don't be sold like slaves'.

**12.10**
Someone has just said that the magistrates have read the Riot Act! This means that if people don't go away within an hour they will be arrested. However, there seems to be great confusion here. Most people do not seem to have heard that the Riot Act has been read. The meeting is going on as normal.

**1.20**
Henry Hunt has arrived at the meeting. He climbed on to the platform from which he was to speak and said, 'Gentlemen, I must ask you to be peaceful, a great deal depends upon that, and I trust that all who hear me will remain quiet.'

**1.30**
There is real trouble here now. The cavalry have just charged at the demonstrators.

**1.35**
I have just received a picture drawn by an onlooker.

**1.40**
There is panic everywhere. No-one seems to know what has happened. A man who writes for *The Times* newspaper told me he was listening to Hunt speak when the cavalry rushed through the crowd with swords drawn and grabbed Henry Hunt. He says the meeting would have been very peaceful if this had not happened.
   Another reporter who works for the *Courier* told me that when Hunt was arrested, the mob attacked the cavalry and threw missiles at them. The cavalry had to protect themselves. There is a big argument about who started the trouble!

**1.45**
Samuel Bamford, an eye witness, tells me he saw 'the cavalry cut the people; they sabred or trampled women and children'. He is on the Radicals' side but he also told me he saw several mounds of people, some still groaning, others with staring eyes who were gasping for breath, and others who breathed no more!
   The man from *The Times* who doesn't support the Radicals said, 'The cavalry hurried in all directions, cutting at anyone. A man near me had his nose completely taken off by a blow from a sabre. Nothing was thrown at the soldiers until they attacked.

**1.50**
I have spoken to John Lees who was there. He said, 'When I got to the end of Watson Street, I saw ten or twelve of the cavalry cutting at the people. An officer rode up and stopped them, but when he had gone they started again.'

**2.00**
I have just heard about the casualties. They say eleven people have been killed and 400 wounded. Here are details of three of the hurt.
   Elizabeth Adshead, aged 43, ribs injured when trampled by the crowd. John Ainsworth, aged 24, weaver, sword cut on the right cheek. Thomas Blumstone, aged 74, blacksmith, both arms badly broken.

**2.15**
Everyone is asking who is to blame for the tragedy. The magistrates say that Hunt should be ashamed for the disaster he has created. The demonstrators are saying that they were attacked without reason and it just shows what this country is coming to.
   Some people are sarcastically calling the incident 'Peterloo' after our army's last 'great' victory at Waterloo!

# **W**as 'Peterloo' a massacre?

**O**n 16 AUGUST 1819 a crowd of about 80,000 men, women and children gathered at St Peter's Fields in Manchester. They had come to listen to Henry Hunt, a leading campaigner, talk about parliamentary reform. The meeting was also held to attack government policy.

The local people in charge, the magistrates, were very worried that the whole thing would get out of hand and lead to revolution. They decided to ban the meeting and sent soldiers through the crowd to arrest Hunt. It was a disaster! Either in self defence, or out of panic, or just brutality, the soldiers ended up killing eleven people and wounding over 400, including 113 women. See if you can make up your mind whose fault you think it was.

---

**SOURCE 1** Written by Samuel Bamford in *Passages in the Life of a Radical*, 1839–42

*I stood on tiptoe and saw a party of the cavalry come trotting sword in hand. On the cavalry drawing up in a line they were welcomed with a shout of goodwill, as I understood it. They waved their swords over their heads and striking spur into their horses they dashed forward and began cutting the people.*

*'Stand fast,' I said. 'They are riding upon us; stand fast.' And there was a general cry in our part of the crowd of 'Stand fast'. The cavalry were in confusion: they could not, with all the weight of man and horse, penetrate that compact mass of human beings; and their swords were plied [used] to hew a way through naked held-up hands and defenceless heads; and then chopped limbs and wound-gaping skulls were seen; and groans and cries were mingled with the din of that horrid confusion. 'Ah! ah!' 'For shame! for shame!' was shouted. Then, 'Break! break! They are killing them in the front and they cannot get away'; and there was a general cry of 'Break! break!'*

*On the breaking of the crowd the cavalry wheeled, and dashing whenever there was an opening, they followed, pressing and wounding. Women, white-vested maids and tender youths were indiscriminately cut down or trampled.*

*In ten minutes the field was an open and almost deserted place. Over the field were strewed caps, bonnets and several mounds of human beings where they had fallen, crushed down and smothered.*

---

**SOURCE 2** An account by one of the soldiers

*Up to the point of surrounding the hustings [platform] no violence whatever was used on the part of the cavalry. A shout of defiance was set up against them on their coming on the ground. It has been asserted that the cavalry cut at the mob right and left as they advanced to the hustings. They struck no blow till they were attacked by the mob. Before the cavalry reached the hustings, stones and other missiles were thrown at them and this mode of attack was increased so much that it became necessary in self defence to resist it.*

---

**SOURCE 3** An eyewitness account

*I saw the cavalry, they were scattered and hemmed in by the mob, so that they were powerless. The charge of the cavalry swept this mass of human beings before it. The soldiers drove the people forward with the flats of their swords; but sometimes, as is almost inevitably the case when men are placed in such situations, the edge of the sword was used, but most of the injuries came from the pressure of the mob.*

---

1. Of the three written sources, two seem to agree with each other. Which two are they?
2. Make a list of all the differences between those two sources and the other written source.
3. Does the fact that two of the sources agree mean they are right?

---

*continued* ▶

▶ *continued*

**SOURCE 4**
*Manchester Heroes*, a
cartoon by Cruikshank

**SOURCE 5** A view of St
Peter's Place

4. Now look at Sources 4 and 5. Do they support
   the view that the soldiers deliberately attacked
   the people, or that the soldiers probably
   panicked?
5. Now write your own account of what you think
   happened at St Peter's Fields.

**PEACE & WAR** BRITAIN 1750–1900

# **W**ere the Chartists revolutionaries?

Working in groups, fill in the chart below. You will need to refer to pages 92–94 of your textbook.

1. Make a list of all the different methods the Chartists used.
2. Which, if any, of these could be said to be revolutionary? Explain your answer.
3. Make a list of all the aims of the Chartists.
4. Which of these could be said to be revolutionary? Explain your answer.

5. As a group, reach a conclusion on whether the Chartists were revolutionaries. Be prepared to argue your case in class.

| Methods | Were they revolutionary? | Reasons |
|---|---|---|
|  |  |  |
|  |  |  |
|  |  |  |
|  |  |  |

| Aims | Were they revolutionary? | Reasons |
|---|---|---|
|  |  |  |
|  |  |  |
|  |  |  |
|  |  |  |
|  |  |  |

*letter to the public*

# A LETTER

## "To the Public generally, and to our Neighbours in particular.

"WE, *John Hughes, David Jones* and *John Hugh,* now lying in Cardiff gaol, convicted of the attack on the Pontardulais turnpike gate, and the police stationed there to protect it—being now sentenced to transportation, beg, and earnestly call on others to take warning by our fate, and to stop in their mad course, before they fall into our condemnation.

*"We are guilty and doomed to suffer*, while hundreds have escaped. Let them, and every one, take care not to be deluded again to attack public or private property, and resist the power of the law, for it will overtake them with vengeance, and bring them down to destruction.

"We are only in prison now, but in a week or two shall be banished as rogues—to be slaves to strangers in a strange land. We must go, in the prime of life, from our dear homes, to live and labour with the worst of villains—looked upon as thieves.

"Friends—neighbours—all—but especially young men—keep from night meetings! Fear to do wrong, and dread the terrors of the judge.

"Think of what we *must* and you *may suffer* before you *dare* to do as we have done.

"If you will be peaceable, and live again like honest men, by the blessing of God, you may expect to prosper; and we, poor outcast wretches, may have to thank you for the mercy of the Crown—for on no other terms than your good conduct will any pity be shewn to us, or others, who may fall into our almost hopeless situation.

*(Signed)*

*"JOHN HUGHES,*
*"DAVID JONES,*
*"The X mark of JOHN HUGH.*

"Cardiff Gaol, Nov. 1st, 1843.
  "Witness, John B. Woods, Governor."

**SOURCE 1** An open letter to the public from three men transported to Australia for taking part in the Rebecca Riots

1. What is this letter asking people to do?
2. Do you think that this letter was really written by the three men?
3. Write here the reasons for your answers to question 2.

_____

_____

_____

_____

_____

_____

# Census form: Shelton Street

| Address and floor | Name | Gender | Age | Married or single | Occupation |
|---|---|---|---|---|---|
| | | | | | |
| | | | | | |
| | | | | | |
| | | | | | |
| | | | | | |
| | | | | | |
| | | | | | |
| | | | | | |
| | | | | | |
| | | | | | |
| | | | | | |
| | | | | | |
| | | | | | |

# Death report form: Shelton Street

| Address and floor | Name | Age at death | Cause of death |
|---|---|---|---|
| | | | |
| | | | |
| | | | |
| | | | |

# The Victorians discover history

**SOURCE 1** Written by the American writer Nathaniel Hawthorne in 1862 about the attitude to history of a typical British person

*He likes to feel the weight of all the past upon his back; and, moreover, the antiquity that overburdens him has taken root in his being, and has grown to be rather a hump than a pack, so that there is no getting rid of it without tearing his whole structure to pieces . . . As he appears to be sufficiently comfortable under the mouldy accretion, he had better stumble on with it as long as he can.*

1. Look at Source 1. What attitude does it suggest that many British people in the nineteenth century had towards history?
2. Nathaniel Hawthorne was an American. What in Source 1 suggests that his attitude to history was different from that of British people? What might explain his different attitude?

MANY British people in the nineteenth century were indeed very interested in the past. Never before had people been so aware of, and involved in, their own history. It is thanks to the Victorians that many historic monuments and artefacts, from Roman times or the Middle Ages, for example, were preserved for us to enjoy today. The Victorians founded many museums and set up the National Trust. At the same time, however, the Victorians did not want to allow history to get in the way of 'progress', as they saw it, and so some historic monuments which were 'in the way' were destroyed.

Why were many Victorians so fascinated by history? One possible reason is that they were living through a period of such rapid change. Some people liked to see the changes in their own lifetime as the end of a story of progress stretching back into

history. They wanted to see the present as connected with the past. In some cases, they wanted to emphasise how much better the present was than the past. Other people didn't like many of the changes, or found the new world which had been created a rather worrying place. They tended to romanticise the past and identify with it, and some tried to revive traditional styles. In some cases, they looked to the past to back up their arguments for social or political change.

Sources 2–4 reflect the variety of Victorian attitudes towards history.

3. Look at Sources 2–4. Try to match each source with one of the following captions:
- produced by someone who felt that the present was better than the past
- produced by someone with a 'romantic' view of the past
- produced by someone who saw the present as the end of a story of progress stretching back into history
- produced by someone who wanted to revive traditional styles.

**SOURCE 2** From an essay written by a historian, Thomas Babington Macaulay, in 1835

*. . . Nothing is so interesting and delightful as to contemplate the steps by which the England of Domesday Book, crusaders, monks, serfs, outlaws, became the England we know and love. The Great Charter, the first assembling of the House of Commons, the extinction of personal slavery, the separation from Rome, the Revolution [of 1688], the establishment of the liberty of unlicensed printing, the reform of the representative system, all these seem to me to be the successive stages of one great revolution.*

continued ▶

▶ *continued*

**SOURCE 3** A painting called *The Boyhood of Raleigh*, by Sir John Millais. Sir Walter Raleigh (1552–1618) was one of the leading explorers during the reign of Elizabeth I

**SOURCE 4** A Victorian house built in Tudor style in about 1900

4. Look through your textbook to see if you can find other examples of Victorian attitudes to history.
5. What similarities and differences can you see between Victorian attitudes to history and attitudes to history today?

# THE TWENTIETH-CENTURY WORLD

## Introduction

**The Twentieth-Century World** is the final statutory unit in the Key Stage 3 Programme of Study. You can see from the notes on pages 4–18 how best to meet the requirements of the revised National Curriculum when teaching with this book.

In summary, the unit begins with a brief overview of the First World War. This not only covers the relevant overview requirement of the revised curriculum, but also serves to set up major themes for the subsequent sections: the apportioning of blame for the War, the aftermath of the fighting, and the legacy of the Treaty of Versailles.

Section 2 provides an extended causation exercise on causes of the Second World War.

Sections 3 and 4 look in detail at the experience of war for combatants, for civilians and for wartime leaders.

Section 5 looks briefly at the immediate consequences of the War, a story which will of course be picked up and developed for many pupils in GCSE.

### AIMS OF THIS UNIT

■ Given the shorter chronological span of this unit, change is a less prominent theme than in Britain 1750–1900.

However, there are substantial opportunities throughout the unit for pupils to see changes in action, e.g. how Hitler, Stalin and Mussolini changed life in the countries they ruled, how the experience of war changed people's lives in Britain, or how the War itself changed Europe.

■ The enquiries of Section 2 combine into an extended exercise into the causes of the Second World War.

Pupils are introduced first to a simple causal factor – Hitler's actions. They are then invited to consider a range of less personal factors, which by their very nature are more complex and abstract, e.g. the policy of Appeasement and the failure of the League of Nations.

■ Section 3 of the unit serves two purposes, not only giving pupils the story of some important events of the war, but also emphasising the experience of war. This allows pupils to see what life was like for a wide range of people, both combatant and civilian, and to tackle a depth study on the Home Front during the Second World War.

■ The investigation of historical interpretations is featured in enquiries such as those into Dunkirk (a triumph or a disaster?); the Blitz; the images (public and private) of Hitler and Churchill; and in the key questions behind a number of enquiries, such as those into the Holocaust or the bombing of Dresden, about the nature of war crimes.

■ Source-based enquiry features throughout as always, although a particular aim in this unit is to help pupils to use political cartoons as historical evidence.

### FURTHER READING

A wide range of modern historians are cited in the sources throughout the unit. Any of these can form useful background reading. However, as background to the section on the causes of the War it would be particularly useful for you to read A.J.P. Taylor's *The Origins of the Second World War*, which first advanced the view that Hitler was not wholly responsible for the War. For the opposite viewpoint Alan Bullock's *Hitler: A Study in Tyranny* is the best source. These two works are the origins of the two viewpoints on page 148.

# Detailed notes

## Section 1: 1900–1919

The first three enquiries serve a number of essential purposes:

■ Most obviously, they provide an overview of the First World War.

■ Secondly, they provide a valuable study in causation: looking at the long-term causes and the triggers of the First World War.

■ Thirdly, these enquiries provide a sound basis for pupils to understand what the Programme of Study calls 'the consequences of the First World War' – in particular how the horrific slaughter of the Great War, and the harsh peace terms imposed on Germany by the Treaty of Versailles, were to cast a long shadow across the post-war years.

If your chosen depth studies are to include the Home Front or the Western Front in World War I, you will need to use the parallel publication *Britain and the Great War*.

### ENQUIRY: THE STAGE IS SET FOR WAR

Pupils' Book pp. 110–113
Worksheet 27

This two-spread enquiry not only helps bridge the gap between Britain 1750–1900 and The Twentieth-Century World, but also serves two other purposes which make it worth tackling in its own right.

Firstly, the material provides a useful study in causation. The main long-term factors – colonial rivalry, naval rivalry and the alliance system – and the trigger events are clearly identified and distinguished, and the Activity on page 113 allows them to be contrasted.

Secondly, it prepares for the work on The Twentieth-Century World in a very important way. One of the issues in Section 2, where we examine causes of the Second World War, is the way the Treaty of Versailles laid blame on Germany for the First World War, and the resentment this caused in Germany. This enquiry can be used to investigate the issue of who, if anyone, was responsible, without pupils knowing who later got the blame. The Activity at the end of the enquiry focuses on this, and pupils are asked to reach their own conclusion. Later, as they consider the terms and consequences of the Treaty of Versailles, they can be reminded of the conclusion they reached here.

(Pages 110–111)

### 'To be a great country you must colonise'

The three quotations which introduce each of these sub-sections are genuine. You could write all three of them prominently on the board to structure your work on long-term causes (pages 110–112). This first one is from a speech by a French politician.

**Question 1:** This builds naturally on work done in Unit A on Britain's overseas Empire. The answer is probably France and Britain, although Germany, from almost nothing pre-1870, had built up a moderately large empire by 1914.

### 'Our future lies on the ocean'

This second quotation is from a speech by Kaiser Wilhelm of Germany.

**Sources 2 and 4:** *Dreadnought* was the name of the first ship, but it then became a generic name for the new battleships.

(Pages 112–113)

### 'The division of the great powers . . .'

**Question 1:** You could provide a grid for pupils to complete.

### 28 June 1914 – the spark!

You might like to tell pupils the story of the events of 28 June in greater detail. It was a fascinating mix of good planning and luck which finally led to Gavrilo Princip being in a position to shoot the Archduke and his wife from close range. See, for example, the account in *Britain at War* by Craig Mair, published by John Murray (pages 18–20).

**Activity: Worksheet 27** helps pupils organise their thoughts in preparation for this activity.

It is also essential as preparation for this activity (particularly questions 3 and 4) that pupils consider the trigger events (Source 7) in the context of the longer-term causes. A class discussion around the following questions should be useful: If the longer-term causes had not been present, would the triggers have had the same effect? If they were present, but the assassination had not happened, would a war of some kind still have been inevitable?

### ENQUIRY: A NEW KIND OF WARFARE

Pupils' Book pp. 114–115

This single-spread enquiry provides a very brief account of the First World War. If you are intending to cover this topic as a depth study, the separate book in this series, *Britain and the Great War*, by Greg Hetherton, must be used.

The main purpose of this spread is to give pupils some idea of the terrible nature of the War, especially the very high casualty figures. This is important for later work. The memory of it was, and is, part of the legacy of the Great War, and it was one reason for many politicians' determination to avoid another war at almost any cost. The Activity on page 115 focuses on this theme.

**Source 1:** Some time could be spent in studying Nevinson's painting carefully. There is a wealth of detail to be found.

The Imperial War Museum publication *Images of the First World War*, which contains work by dozens of war artists, could be used to extend this activity.

## ENQUIRY: WAS THE TREATY OF VERSAILLES A MISTAKE? PART ONE

Pupils' Book pp. 116–117
Worksheet 28

This single-spread enquiry looks at the terms of the Treaty of Versailles and the seeds of future problems which it sowed.

It attempts to lay out as clearly as possible both the terms of the Treaty of Versailles and the motives of the people involved. Some of the consequences are hinted at here, but they are not fully developed. We return to the Treaty and its consequences on pages 136–137.

**Worksheet 28** provides a simulation exercise on the Versailles negotiations. If you decide to use this exercise (and it does help to reinforce pupils' understanding of what the issues were and of what happened) it needs to be used *before* pupils have worked through pages 116–117 of the Pupils' Book. Don't hand out the book, therefore. Instead, hand out the three-page worksheet. On the first page pupils will find the information in the left-hand column of page 116 and instructions for the simulation. The second and third pages, 'Problems', can be given to pupils as they stand, or can be cut into three so that each group sees only its own problems. This could make the activity more accessible. The third page is also a record sheet for each group to complete.

The exercise is based around three groups of four pupils. However, your class is probably somewhat larger than twelve! Simply have more than one group work on each set of problems (two different groups of four working on each set of problems would keep every pupil in a class of 24 busy). Alternatively, have just three groups, but eight pupils in each group, with pairs of pupils representing each politician.

Stress to pupils that they must consider the problems from the point of view of the person/country they are representing.

For questions 5 and 6 on the worksheet you might want to take control and chair the discussions. You could draw the final agreed version of the treaty on the board.

Question 8 allows for each pupil to write a piece of work of their own; this could be used for assessment purposes if you wish. However, we all know that some pupils show an understanding through their contributions to discussion that they rarely show in their written work. This simulation therefore provides a good opportunity for listening in on the group discussions and using this oral evidence for recording purposes. You might only be able to do this with one or two groups. Members of the other groups could be assessed on another occasion, when they are working in groups again.

One last point: it is important to ensure that at the end of the exercise pupils are clear about what the *actual* terms of the Treaty of Versailles were, as opposed to the terms which they arrived at during their own simulations. This is one important purpose behind question 9.

### The aims

**Source 1:** The main protagonists, Wilson, Clemenceau and Lloyd George, are shown at the centre of the painting. The artist is on record as being thoroughly disillusioned by what he saw and heard at Versailles. Pupils might consider the attitude he has attributed to each of the three main signatories.

### The terms

**Question 1:** Pupils have already made a judgement about who was most to blame for the First World War, on page 113. These judgements, and any disagreements around the class, could form the starting point for attempting this question.

**Question 1:** Pupils could work in groups of six and take one set of terms each.

## Section 2: The causes of the Second World War

It will be clear to pupils from the enquiries in Section 1 that the First World War and the Treaty of Versailles created new problems for Europe, rather than solving the old ones. The mess that was left after the War, the horror at the slaughter, and the economic and political crises in Europe that followed in its wake, were all important ingredients of the growth of dictatorships in Europe. They were thus all long-term causes of the Second World War.

This section therefore begins with a study of the rise of the dictators in the USSR, Italy and Germany. The initial focus is on the domestic scene in each country, but pupils are also able to reach their own provisional opinion on how far the dictators threatened peace in Europe. Pupils are also introduced to Hitler.

Against this background, the rest of the section looks at the overall international scene, in a sustained examination of the causes of the Second World War. Our main aim is to show pupils that causal explanations are by their very nature problematic. The strategy used to do this involves first of all looking at events between 1933 and 1939, with an emphasis on the actions of Hitler, in the enquiry *Hitler's war*. By examining Hitler's moves in military rearmament and foreign policy, pupils will clearly see his responsibility for the outbreak of the Second World War.

Having set up this interpretation, the later enquiries then question how satisfactory such a simple 'personal' explanation is by looking at other causal factors – the policy of Appeasement, the Treaty of Versailles again, the role of the USA, the USSR and the League of Nations, and finally the rise of Japan – with the emphasis on the more 'impersonal' causal factors.

It is hoped that this approach will help pupils gradually to develop an understanding of some of the complexities involved in looking for a causal explanation of the War. It should also help them to understand that historical explanations are always provisional, and that when an event or a series of events is looked at using fresh evidence, or from a different perspective, a revised explanation will result.

The focus throughout this section is clearly on causation, but as with all history it is impossible and indeed undesirable to leave out other areas.

(With thanks to Tim Lomas for ideas and material provided for *Hitler's war*.)

## ENQUIRY: THE RISE OF THE DICTATORS

Pupils' Book pp. 118–123
Worksheets 29, 30, 31, 32

This three-spread enquiry attempts:
■ briefly to cover the rise of dictators in the USSR, Italy and Germany
■ to help pupils develop an understanding of the main characteristics of these dictatorships, and the differences between dictatorships and democracies
■ to allow pupils to understand how certain features in these dictatorships posed dangers for international peace.

In discussing the general differences between a democracy and a dictatorship we have started by building on pupils' prior understanding of Britain in the nineteenth century from their study of Unit A. However, our general approach in this enquiry has not been to compare structural differences between democracies and dictatorships, but rather to focus on what it is like to live under these different systems.

An alternative way to introduce this enquiry would be to study different democracies and dictatorships today. There are obviously opportunities here for the cross-curricular theme of Citizenship.

(Pages 118–119)

**Question 1:** This is a general question that runs behind everything in the enquiry. You will need to use it for class discussion after each of the case studies.

### Case study 1: the USSR

**Question 3:** Pupils are expected to base their answers on the background information in the case study.

**Question 4:** You might refer them in particular to their study of Victorian values on pages 64–69.

### Case study 2: Italy

**Question 1:** Make sure pupils look at positive aspects of each regime, e.g. improving industry or health care, as well as negatives, such as treatment of opponents.

(Pages 120–121)

### Case study 3: Germany – why did Hitler rise to power?

This brief survey of the rise of Hitler may need amplification. You might also want to use a timeline while you are telling this story.

**Sources 5–12:** We have left detailed interrogation up to you.

**Worksheet 29** is extension work on the nature of Hitler's regime and the reasons people had for supporting him. It provides a single long written source, which serves as a useful summary of events in Germany from the point of view of an ordinary German.

(Pages 122–123)

### What was life like in Nazi Germany?

**Question 1:** Encourage pupils to support their view using evidence in the narrative or in Sources 13–18. **Worksheet 30** (two pages) has been provided to help pupils organise their research for this question. It will also provide a useful starting point for the Activity.

**Activity: Worksheet 31** provides a report form for filling in the information in the three categories.

The Activity gives an opportunity for extended writing. Using the evidence they have gathered, pupils might conclude that an alliance is possible between any two of them, but perhaps unlikely between all three.

**Worksheet 32** is an investigation of the conflict between dictatorship and democracy in Spain. The sequence of events was as follows. The Republican government appealed for help to the League of Nations, but the two key members, Britain and France, set up a Committee of Non-intervention to prevent foreign help being given to either side. Germany, Italy and the USSR joined the Committee, but ignored its measures. Germany sent 16,000 troops and Italy 50,000 to fight for the Nationalists. Both countries sent tanks and aeroplanes. Stalin sent weapons and advisers to the Republicans. The only other international help the Republicans received was from volunteers, who formed the International Brigade to fight the spread of Fascism. After three years of bloody civil war, including ferocious bombing of civilians and massacres on both sides, Franco won.

Pupils will need to use inference to work out which country some of the sources come from.

You could prepare the grid for question 3 for them.

## ENQUIRY: HITLER'S WAR

Pupils' Book pp. 124–131
Worksheet 32

This four-spread enquiry introduces the rest of the section. It focuses first on what Hitler wrote and said about *Lebensraum*, about German expansion, about the

Treaty of Versailles, about Communism and about his social creed.

It then gives pupils a clear chronological account of the important events from 1933 to 1939: German rearmament and the subsequent territorial conquests. The chronology is reinforced by the timeline which runs across the top of pages 127–131. Particular events on the timeline are illustrated through cartoons or photographs on the rest of the page.

Most of the questions 'en route' are concerned with examining the pictorial sources. How many of them you use and how you use them is entirely up to you. However, note one important aim behind the pupil work we have provided, which is to introduce pupils to the use of political cartoons. Cartoons can present pupils with problems, but this is not a good reason to avoid them, especially at this stage of Key Stage 3, and especially because this period abounds with excellent cartoons which represent so well how events looked to the people living through them.

Throughout the notes on the rest of this enquiry we have provided detailed information about individual cartoons to help you support the pupils' examination and discussion of the cartoons. If pupils are guided through the cartoons in this way you can help them acquire a distinct skill which will stand them in good stead for the rest of the unit.

It is also worth reiterating some important general principles:

■ Cartoons must, of course, be seen in their historical context, and that is how they are used here. Pupils should be encouraged to use what they know about the historical context to interpret and evaluate the cartoons. They should not be used in a content vacuum.

■ A cartoon tells us much about the assumptions and attitudes of the people to whom it was addressed. Cartoons would not be effective or funny if they were viewed by contemporary readers as foolish or wicked. A series of cartoons can also tell us how assumptions and attitudes were changing during a period.

■ Cartoons can also be useful for telling us about:
a) the ideas which the cartoonists were seeking to put over
b) the ideas of the newspaper owners, editors, etc. who allowed the cartoons to be published
c) in some cases, what governments were anxious for people to believe.

We do need to be careful when applying the principles in b) and c) above. No cartoonist or newspaper in Hitler's Germany or in Stalin's Soviet Union would have dared to go against the wishes of the government. But in other countries, such as Britain, cartoons were produced which were highly embarrassing to the government. Low's cartoons, of which we have reproduced several, are good examples of this. In fact, Low's cartoons for the *Evening Standard* in the 1930s show how careful we have to be before drawing conclusions from cartoons. The fact that the *Evening Standard* published Low's anti-Nazi cartoons on a regular basis does not mean that they represented the editorial line of the newspaper. The owner, Lord Beaverbrook, actually took a sympathetic attitude towards Hitler, and he wrote about Low in 1938, 'Brilliant in drawing, inexhaustible in invention – and, mostly, wrong in viewpoint.' However, Low's cartoons looked all the stronger for being in Beaverbrook's paper. Low drew what he wanted and there was little editorial interference.

The cartoon below is one of the few which did invite editorial interference. It shows Hitler as a ventriloquist performing for Chamberlain with Mussolini as his doll. It was drawn in November 1936, but was never used in the paper. The editor wrote to Low, 'We have talked over the ventriloquist cartoon very carefully, and have decided to hold it over for the present for this reason: we do not want at the present time to run what will seem to be a cartoonist's campaign against the dictators. I suggest, therefore, that for the present you avoid the dictators altogether.'

The notes on individual cartoons owe a great debt to the commentary in an excellent collection of cartoons, *Between the Wars 1919–1939: The cartoonists' vision*, by Roy Douglas.

THE JAW IS THE JAW OF MUSSO, BUT—

(Pages 124–125)

## What Hitler wrote and said

**Question 1**: You could limit some pupils to one source. There are varying degrees of complexity: Source 1 is very easy, Sources 2 and 5 much more difficult. Alternatively, this could be a brainstorm activity, with pairs of pupils being asked to look at one source each.

**Question 2**: Notice in particular the consistent commitment to enlarging Germany to provide additional living space.

(Pages 126–127)

## What Hitler did: rearmament

We now turn to Hitler's actions.

You might need to explain what Hitler and Germany were doing getting involved in the Spanish Civil War (see 1937 in the small timeline). **Worksheet 32** is extension material on the Spanish Civil War. It looks at the ideological conflict between Fascism and Communism that lay behind the involvement of foreign dictatorships and democracies in this civil war.

**Activity:** This could be a wide ranging activity. Pupils will need to refer back to the Treaty of Versailles to see what restrictions were placed on German armaments. Pupils will need to consider in their speech:
- what rearmament has taken place (see timeline)
- how this rearmament is reversing the unfair terms of Versailles
- how other powers have been rearming as well, in a way that may threaten German security.

## What Hitler did: foreign policy

The timeline is intended to give a strong chronological drive to these pages. The chronology is further underpinned by a later summary spread, *How did the Second World War happen?*

For the five steps to war, i.e. each of Hitler's territorial actions, both the reasons he gave and the reactions of the rest of Europe are given.

**Source 11:** This cartoon was published in the *Los Angeles Times*, 2 March 1936, when the French–Soviet Pact was being negotiated. The cartoonist obviously approves of the Pact as a way of encircling Germany and preventing military expansion to both the east (the figure of Russia) and the west (the figure of France). The curved surface (representing the whole earth) and the fact that this is an American cartoon show that the Nazis were seen as a world, not just a European, threat.

**Source 12:** This will be compared with Sources 13 and 18.

(Pages 128–129)

**Source 14:** This cartoon is from *Punch*, 23 February 1938. Hitler is portrayed as a poacher. He has just killed 'Austrian integrity', shown as a chamois (an Alpine deer). Mussolini is a corrupt gamekeeper who does not intend to interfere with his friend's activities (Mussolini had agreed not to oppose the *Anschluss*). The cartoon is probably set in the South Tyrol, an area which contained many German speakers but had been given to Italy by the peace treaties of 1919. Hitler agreed not to claim the South Tyrol if Mussolini turned a blind eye to the *Anschluss*.

**Source 15:** This cartoon comes from the Nazi magazine *Simplicissimus*, published in Munich, 3 April 1938. It is entitled 'The fulfilment'. It reflects the German government's view about the *Anschluss*. German troops are marching into an Austrian village, where they are enthusiastically welcomed. The caption reflects the thoughts of one of the Austrians, perhaps the one with the pipe.

**Source 16:** This cartoon was published in the *News of the World* on 25 September 1938, after Chamberlain's first two meetings with Hitler, but before the final meeting in Munich. It shows Chamberlain trying to steer the world safely along the cracking plank 'Czech crisis' from 'Chaos' to 'Peace'. You can see the jagged rock 'War' underneath the plank. This represents the danger of Chamberlain failing. The cartoon emphasises the enormous personal responsibility Chamberlain had in the matter.

**Source 17:** This cartoon comes from a leading Nazi newspaper, *Völkischer Beobachter*, published in Munich, 13 October 1938. Surprisingly, it is part of an advertisement for a book of sketches. The characters are 'regulars' at a café table; the sourceline gives the chronology of the events they are responding to. In the first frame they are eagerly celebrating their government's action at the beginning of the crisis. However, in the next two pictures they become alarmed and then frightened when war becomes likely. Their spirits are revived in the final picture by the news of the Munich settlement. The cartoon suggests that there was fear and worry about possible war in Germany (as there was elsewhere in Europe) during this crisis.

(Pages 130–131)

**Source 19:** This cartoon was published in the *Evening Standard*, 2 November 1939, and is by David Low. It is entitled 'Someone is Taking Someone for a Walk'. It clearly shows Low's doubts about how long the Pact would last.

**Source 21:** This cartoon comes from the *Daily Express*, 6 September 1939, just after the Second World War began. It suggests that Hitler had not intended such a war to break out and that he was caught by surprise by Britain and France's declaration of war. It is a matter for debate whether Hitler really did think that he could fight and defeat Poland without Britain and France intervening.

**Question 7:** This serves as a summary question, getting pupils to consider cartoons as a particular type of historical source material. However, we emphasise that any discussion of the usefulness of cartoons should always be focused on particular cartoons – in this case the nine on pages 118–131. Pupils should not be encouraged to think that there are general statements that can be learned about all cartoons, e.g. all cartoons are biased, or cartoons are of no use because they are only designed to make people laugh. Pupils should instead be encouraged to use and evaluate each cartoon on its own unique merits for a particular given purpose.

**Activity:** The four points to be considered are: (i) begin cautiously, (ii) pretend to be stronger than you are, (iii) wait for chances, and create opportunities by stirring up trouble, (iv) be fast and decisive even if in doubt. Pupils can supplement their work on each theme by their own research in the school library if they are willing.

### Hitler's war?

**Question 1:** Display the terms on the board, or summarise each one on a separate card.

**Question 3:** This invites a response based on the information the pupils have been given. It is a provisional conclusion and will be revised in the light of subsequent evidence in the later enquiries.

## ENQUIRY: WAS APPEASEMENT A MISTAKE?

Pupils' Book pp. 132–135
Worksheet 34

On pages 132–147 we are going to investigate other factors which contributed to the outbreak of the Second World War.

This two-spread enquiry addresses a question still hotly debated by historians: whether the policy of appeasing Hitler was a mistake.

(Pages 132–133)

### Arguments for Appeasement/Arguments against Appeasement

**Source 2:** This Low cartoon appeared in the *Evening Standard* on 5 October 1938, shortly after Chamberlain brought home from Munich an agreement with Hitler which referred to 'the desire of our two peoples never to go to war with one another again. We are resolved that consultation shall be the method adopted to deal with questions that may concern our two countries.' On the left are the figures of Chamberlain, Sir John Simon (Chancellor of the Exchequer) and Lord Halifax (Foreign Secretary). They appear to be frolicking like lambs for joy about the agreement. On the right John Bull is rather more doubtful, but Lord Beaverbrook reassures him.

**Question 1:** The arguments defending and criticising Appeasement need to be discussed carefully in class before tackling this question. Various strategies might be:

■ to make cards summarising the main point of each argument and photocopy these for each pupil
■ to give pupils five minutes to read one argument each and then summarise it on a card themselves.

The evidence about how prepared Britain and Germany were for war can be misleading. The following figures illustrate this:

|  | Annual military aircraft production, 1935–41 | | | |
|---|---|---|---|---|
|  | **Britain** | **France** | **Germany** | |
|  | Total | Total | Total | (non-combat) |
| 1935 | 1440 | 785 | 3183 | (1360) |
| 1936 | 1877 | 890 | 5112 | (3538) |
| 1937 | 2153 | 743 | 5606 | (2955) |
| 1938 | 2825 | 1382 | 5235 | (1885) |
| 1939 | 7940 | 3163 | 8295 | (3562) |
| 1940 | 15,049 | 2441 | 10,247 | |
| 1941 | 20,094 | – | 11,776 | |

The totals appear at first glance to show that Germany was producing more aircraft throughout the 1930s. But many of the German aircraft produced were non-combat aircraft, used for training pilots and transport duties. The numbers in brackets show how many of the German aircraft were of this type.

There are other questions which need to be asked about these figures, e.g. about the quality of the aircraft, and the number of properly trained pilots.

It is also worth considering whether the rapid expansion of British aircraft production between 1936 and 1939 shows that Chamberlain's rearmament plans worked.

**Questions 2–3:** Pupils should consider as many of Sources 3–11 as they can, deciding which side of the argument each source supports. It is certainly recommended that you start this process by discussing Sources 1 and 2 in class, although some pupils may need help with other sources as well. For some pupils you could limit the number of sources to be used to five or six.

If you have made summaries of each argument on cards they can be used here. First, ask pupils working in pairs to collect together the arguments which support Appeasement, and those which oppose Appeasement. Then one person in each pair should identify which of Sources 3–11 can be used to support Appeasement, and the other person should identify those which can be used to criticise it. Pupils will find this easier if they can physically move the arguments around.

If you wanted to make the task harder you could then ask pupils to use each of Sources 1–11 to support one of the particular arguments for or against Appeasement.

(Pages 134–135)

### For or against Appeasement?

**Source 9:** This cartoon is from the Communist *Daily Worker* of 1 October 1938, immediately after the Munich Agreement. It is significant because it can probably be taken to represent the views of the Soviet government. Look at the expression on Chamberlain's face. He appears to have been completely duped by Hitler and Mussolini into signing a document entitled 'Axis Strengthening Agreement'. Daladier appears to be rather uncertain about what he has just done, but his signature is on the document. Hitler and Mussolini look very pleased with themselves, but it is doubtful whether Mussolini was really pleased. Italy gained nothing from the agreement, while Germany continued to grow stronger. However, Mussolini was relieved that war had been averted, because Italy was totally unprepared.

**Question 1:** It might be best to direct pupils to Sources 5, 6, 7 and 8.

**Question 2:** This presents an opportunity for some extended writing. The completed essays should then be used in a class debate, with two pupils who have written in support of Appeasement and two who have opposed it speaking for two minutes each. Anyone in the class can then contribute ideas from their essay to the debate.

**Worksheet 34** will help pupils see Appeasement within the wider context of British leadership between the wars, but is better used after the League of Nations has been studied on pages 142–145.

### ENQUIRY: WAS THE TREATY OF VERSAILLES A MISTAKE? PART TWO

Pupils' Book pp. 136–137

This single-spread enquiry completes the examination of the long-term significance of the Treaty of Versailles which we began on page 116. It is clear from these sources that Hitler was not the only German who regarded Versailles as an insult and an injustice that had to be put right. It is also clear that it was not just Germans who had doubts about Versailles. The focus of this enquiry is to ask whether criticisms of Versailles depend on hindsight.

**Source 3:** A German cartoon from the magazine *Simplicissimus*.

**Source 4:** This cartoon is also from *Simplicissimus* and was published in Munich on 24 June 1919. It is entitled 'Consolation'. It is an exaggeration of the real state of affairs, but there was genuine hunger in Germany immediately after the War. More importantly, the cartoon reflects German resentment over reparations.

**Source 5:** This cartoon was published in the Labour *Daily Herald* on 17 May 1919. The 'Big Four' emerge from the Peace Conference: (left to right) Lloyd George, Prime Minister Orlando of Italy, Clemenceau and Wilson. Behind the pillar is the weeping child which Clemenceau is referring to. The child represents the class of people who will be of military age in 1940.

**Source 6:** This cartoon was published in the *Daily Express* on 7 May 1919, while the peace negotiations were still going on. The cartoon is entitled *'Der Tag!'*

('The Day'). This refers to a common belief in Britain at the time that before 1914 German officers used to toast 'The Day', i.e. the day when their country would embark on a victorious war against Britain. Here, Allied statesmen are seen gleefully feeding unpalatable peace terms to a reluctant jackbooted German. The statesmen are (left to right) Lloyd George, Orlando, Clemenceau and Woodrow Wilson. They all seem to be taking great delight in Germany's discomfiture. The hand firmly holding Germany represents the five principal Allies.

**Question 4:** Source 4 is of particular significance here, but other sources also show reservations about Versailles as early as 1919.

### ENQUIRY: DID THE USA AND THE USSR LET EUROPE DOWN?

Pupils' Book pp. 138–141

This two-spread enquiry introduces two more factors which may have contributed to the outbreak of war: what the two most powerful countries in the world were doing while Europe slid into war. The focus is on the Nazi–Soviet Pact and on America's isolationism.

(Pages 138–139)

#### The USSR: the Nazi–Soviet Pact

Pupils have already come across the Nazi–Soviet Pact, but only as one step in a whole series of events leading to war. Here they are given the opportunity to examine the motives of Hitler, and in particular Stalin, in more detail. It is easy to criticise Stalin for signing the Pact, and we point out the advantages it gave Germany on this spread. But it is just as important to view the Pact from a Soviet perspective, and Sources 3 and 5 are particularly important for this. It will help if pupils are also reminded that the USSR was excluded from the Munich negotiations and the agreement concerning the future of the Sudetenland.

**Activity:** it would be useful to use a word processor for this exercise.

(Pages 140–141)

#### Was the USA isolationist?

This spread poses two basic questions: how isolationist the USA actually was, and how important this was in the events leading to war. How isolationist America was is a matter of debate, and we include points from both sides of the argument. The international conferences and agreements in which the USA was involved were the Washington Naval Agreement, 1922 (which limited the number of battleships and cruisers), a 1930 agreement limiting the number of cruisers, and the 1928 Kellogg–Briand Pact, which renounced war as a way of settling disputes.

**Source 7:** This cartoon is from the *Chicago Tribune* of 19 July 1936. The *Tribune* was considered to stand on the far right of American politics. The figure looming over the table and labelled 'European cannon fodder' represents the people of Europe. Their willingness to fight made the First World War possible, but they should now go on strike against any future war which the statesmen might try and drag them into. The writing on the briefcases of the statesmen shows their hypocrisy.

### Did America's isolationism matter?

**Source 9** comes from *Punch*, 10 December 1919. The cartoon shows the 'League of Nations Bridge', with a stone for each of the principal member countries. A sign proudly proclaims that the bridge was designed by the President of the USA, referring to Woodrow Wilson's leading role in setting up the League during the peace negotiations. But 'Uncle Sam', representing the US government, far from adding the keystone that would complete the bridge and hold it firm, is using it as a pillow while he smokes and generally minds his own business.

## ENQUIRY: WHY DID THE LEAGUE OF NATIONS FAIL?

Pupils' Book pp. 142–145
Worksheets 33, 34

This two-spread enquiry investigates the effectiveness of the League of Nations. This is done in two ways, first by looking at the structural weaknesses of the League, and second by using the Italian invasion of Abyssinia as a case study of the League in action.

(Pages 142–143)

### The organisation of the League

**Question 1:** The weaknesses of the League revealed by Source 3 include the USA never becoming a member, Germany and the USSR not joining for some time, and Italy, Japan and Germany later leaving the League.

Other structural weaknesses to be spotted in Source 4 include the fact that decision making was shared between two bodies; the infrequency of meetings (the Council three times a year, the Assembly once a year), which made it difficult to react immediately to problems; the fact that decisions had to be unanimous; and the League's lack of any armed forces of its own. Pupils should be encouraged to try and explain *why* each of these was a weakness, rather than just identifying each one.

**Worksheet 33** looks at the issue of disarmament in the context of the work of the League.

### The League in action: Italy and Abyssinia

**Question 1:** Before attempting this question pupils should carefully consider the background information

and sources on page 143. The inconsistent position of Britain and France (Source 8) needs to be emphasised.

**Source 8:** It might be necessary to discuss this source with pupils.

(Pages 144–145)

### The League's response

**Questions 1 and 2** are more complex and worthwhile questions than they might first appear. If pupils are really beginning to understand the way the League had to work, they will be able to indicate pros and cons for each of the possible courses of action.

**Activity:** This is a central question. Pupils should be encouraged to go through the material carefully first and draw up a list of supporting evidence for each possible explanation.

**Worksheet 34:** 'Weak leadership' is a recurrent criticism of Britain during the 1930s. This worksheet provides a multiple choice quiz that should help pupils assess what decisions they might have made under the same circumstances. The actions Britain actually took were 1a), 2a), 3c), 4c), 5c) and 6b).

### The consequences of the League's failure

**Source 16:** This German cartoon from *Simplicissimus* was published in Munich on 24 May 1936. It shows the League of Nations represented as a senile old man who has just been woken from his sleep. Victorious Italy is shown as a gloating Greek warrior telling the League not to bother about Abyssinia since the Italian army has dealt with the problem.

**Activity:** Germany might at first appear to pupils to have had little direct interest in the outcome of the Abyssinian war. However, defeat for Mussolini would have removed a rival to German interests in central Europe. On the other hand, as Sources 16–18 suggest, Hitler probably learned lessons from the crisis about the ineffectiveness of the League.

## ENQUIRY: THE RISE OF JAPAN

Pupils' Book pp. 146–147

This single-spread enquiry attempts to redress the imbalance found in some textbooks about this period. It shows that at the same time as the stormclouds were gathering over Europe, a similar trend can be found in Asia with the rise of Japan. The USA's natural concern about this development partly explains its lack of interest in events in Europe.

The two main points emphasised in this enquiry are:
■ that the rise of Japan, and its aggressive policy in Eastern Asia, are arguably just as important as German actions and ambitions in Europe
■ that there were two separate wars, one mainly happening in Europe and one in East Asia, until late 1941, when they combined to form a world war.

The first of these two points does raise issues of interpretation, e.g. why it is that British textbooks devote more space to the war in Europe and the struggle with Germany, while many textbooks used in American schools devote more space to the war in Asia and the struggle with Japan. The following example is typical: *The Story of America*, a textbook used widely in the USA, devotes fifteen pages to 'The European War' and nineteen pages to 'The Pacific War', while *Twentieth-Century History* by Tony Howarth, a British textbook, gives these two topics eighteen pages and four pages respectively. Thus two very different versions of the War are created.

We continue the story of the war in Asia on pages 180–181 (*Why did the Japanese attack Pearl Harbor?*) and pages 198–201 (*Was the dropping of the atomic bombs justified?*)

**Question 1:** From left to right, the League, China, Japan, the USSR. What looks like a pot plant on the windowsill is in fact a powder keg, with many fuses and a label saying 'Caution powder'.

**Summary question 1:** It might help pupils if they first draw a timeline and mark on it the main events mentioned on this spread.

### ENQUIRY: HOW DID THE SECOND WORLD WAR HAPPEN?

Pupils' Book pp. 148–149
Worksheets 35, 36

This single-spread enquiry has been designed to help pupils form an overall picture of the events of 1919–1939.

**Question 2:** this is supported by **Worksheets 35 and 36** (which has three pages). The aim of these worksheets is to take pupils through this fairly complex analysis of causation in a highly structured way.

There are two ways to use the worksheets, according to the abilities of your pupils.
■ For more able pupils: simply give them **Worksheet 35.** They can compare the list they have compiled in answer to question 1 on page 148 with the causes on the worksheet.

In their books they should then answer questions 2a) and b) on page 148 as pieces of extended writing. They can also be asked to explain which causes were the most important.
■ For most of the pupils:
Photocopy Worksheet 35 onto thickish paper or card and then cut it up to make one set of cards for each pupil (although see note below). You could, of course, give each pupil a worksheet and let them do the cutting up themselves.

The rest of the exercise is clear from the pupil instructions on Worksheet 36. Pupils select the cards which they think give sensible – i.e. helpful – explanations of the outbreak of the War. They copy

these into the left-hand column of the first page. They then explain the choice in the right-hand column.

N.B. You may wish to restrict some pupils to just these stages, i.e. questions 1–4 on the first page of Worksheet 36. For some pupils you may also wish to simplify the exercise by using only some of the sixteen cause cards from Worksheet 35.

On the second page of the worksheet pupils add any other causes they can think of and explain each one.

Finally, they copy two cards which they think do not help to explain why there was a War, and write down why these are not helpful explanations.

Question 8 on Worksheet 36 adds a new dimension to the exercise, as pupils look at connections between the causes.

Finally, in questions 9–11 on Worksheet 36, pupils think about the relative importance of causes.

Worksheet 35 can also be used to look at triggers and long-term causes.

**Question 3** on page 148 is best dealt with through class discussion.

**Questions 4 and 5:** These could be introduced through class or group discussion, but pupils should then be encouraged to attempt to answer these questions by themselves.

# Section 3: What was life like during the War?

This next section of the book covers various aspects of the Second World War. It gives scope for teaching in outline or in depth, as summarised in the introduction (pages 8–9).

Whichever depth studies you choose to tackle, it would not be satisfactory to leave pupils with just isolated impressions of what life was like during the War. It is important that they should be given the opportunity to develop an overall picture of the chronology of the War, and some knowledge of the most important landmarks. We have therefore arranged these enquiries in chronological order.

This chronology of the War is reinforced by the first enquiry in this section, *The Second World War*, which aims to summarise the overall picture and provide the context for the events studied on the subsequent spreads.

Many of the other enquiries serve both to raise important historical questions in their own right (e.g. *Dunkirk: triumph or disaster?*) and to provide pupils with some of the main landmarks in the story of the War. Of course, which landmarks to cover and which to leave out is an important historical issue in itself, but we have chosen Dunkirk, the Battle of Britain, the invasion of the USSR, the Battle of the Atlantic, the attack on Pearl Harbor, the bombing of Dresden and the dropping of the atomic bombs.

(With thanks to Peter Mantin for ideas and material provided for pages 186–201.)

## ENQUIRY: THE SECOND WORLD WAR

Pupils' Book pp. 150–151
Worksheets 37, 45

This single-spread enquiry provides maps and a timeline which are meant either to provide an overview into which to fit your depth study or for reference if you are tackling a number of World War II enquiries. Question 1 can lead to some lively disagreement. For example, an American, a British and a Soviet historian might well disagree about where these headings should go.

The events we are going to study in detail are starred in the timeline.

**Question 1:** This might be best answered after all the material on the War has been studied. Alternatively, it can be attempted at this stage and then looked at again after the enquiry on the atomic bombs (pages 198–201). **Worksheet 37** is a copy of the timeline for pupils to write on.

**Worksheet 45** is a sequencing exercise which picks up the ideas in question 1. It is used at the end of this section, after pages 198–201.

## ENQUIRY: LIVING THROUGH THE WAR: PART ONE

Pupils' Book pp. 152–157
Worksheets 38, 39

This three-spread enquiry concentrates on the Home Front in Britain just before the War started and during its first year. The focus, therefore, is on preparations for war and evacuation. With *Living through the war: part 2* (pages 164–171) it provides an ideal depth study.

In our study of evacuation the focus is very much on people's attitudes, both to being evacuated themselves and to taking in evacuee families.

(Pages 152–153)

### Evacuation

**Question 1: Worksheet 38** provides a map to support this question. It also repeats questions 1 and 2 so that the worksheet can stand independently of the textbook for homework usage.

The map below shows where the evacuation, reception and neutral areas actually were. This can be compared with the maps pupils have drawn.

**Question 2:** The priority groups were schoolchildren and their teachers (did anyone suggest the latter?), children under five and their mothers, pregnant women and blind and handicapped people.

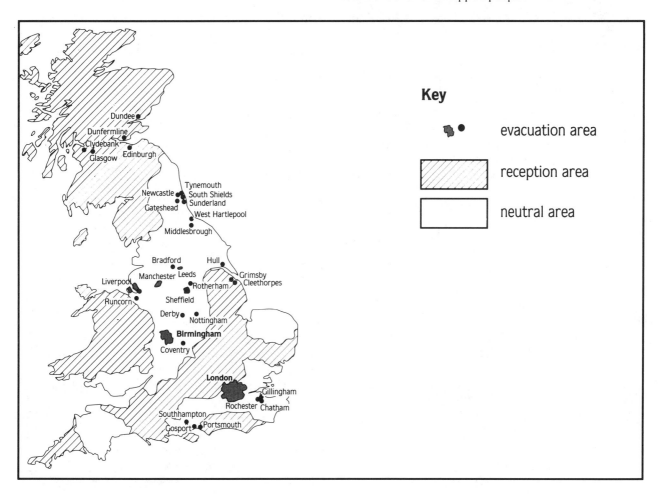

**Key**

- evacuation area
- reception area
- neutral area

**Activity:** the government sent this information to schools about preparing for evacuation:

> Besides the clothes the child is wearing, including an overcoat or mackintosh, a complete change of clothing should be carried. The following is suggested:
>
> | GIRL | BOY |
> | --- | --- |
> | 1 vest or combinations | 1 vest |
> | 1 pair of knickers | 1 shirt with collar |
> | 1 bodice | 1 pair of pants |
> | 1 petticoat | 1 pullover or jersey |
> | 2 pairs of stockings | 1 pair of knickers |
> | Handkerchiefs | Handkerchiefs |
> | Slip and blouse | 2 pairs of socks or |
> | Cardigan | stockings |
>
> All children: nightwear, boots or shoes, comb, plimsolls, towel, soap, face-cloth, toothbrush, gas mask.
>
> Head teachers may use material in needlework lessons to make clothing, bags, towels etc., for children, especially those whose parents are poor.

(Pages 154–155)

**Questions 1–4:** Sources 7–10 should be discussed fully in class. They provide plenty of opportunity for making deductions, and the questions are designed to this end.

(Pages 156–157)

**Source 18:** Pupils may need help in interpreting this.
**Activity:** Sources 11–17 should have been fully discussed in groups or in the whole class beforehand.
You might need to make clear the distinction between working-class experiences and middle-class experiences as shown in the different sources. Sources 11, 12 and 14 are clearly central here, but don't forget to refer pupils back to pages 154–155.
Another approach is to copy out the sources onto cards and ask pupils to separate them into two groups: those from evacuees and those from their hosts. This would also help as preparation for question 4.
**Worksheet 39** gives pupils the opportunity to consider a fictional account of two children's experience of evacuation. It comes from *Carrie's War*, by Nina Bawden. You can read the extracts to the class, but the book is well worth recommending to pupils. These extracts come from the beginning of the story.

## ENQUIRY: DUNKIRK: TRIUMPH OR DISASTER?

Pupils' Book pp. 158–161

This two-spread enquiry focuses on different interpretations of what happened at Dunkirk.

The first set of sources are ones produced at the time of the event, the second set at a later date. This enquiry helps counter the stereotypical view pupils sometimes slip into that the former are not so much interpretations as the latter are. None of them will recount exactly what actually happened; Source 5 is as much an interpretation as Source 12. Nor is it useful to make too much of a distinction between accounts by people involved in the events and accounts by people not involved. Source 10 was written by an eye-witness, but it was not written until the 1960s; it is clearly an interpretation. Source 2 was written by somebody who was not present at Dunkirk, but it was written at the time; it, too, is an interpretation.

(Pages 158–159)

**Blitzkrieg**

It is best to begin by telling pupils the background to Dunkirk, i.e. the story of the *Blitzkrieg*. The animations from the title sequence of *Dad's Army* provide a snappy visual summary of it if you have that available on video.

(Pages 160–161)

**Question 3:** Sources 2–9 come from the time of the event. In preparation for question 3 the class could discuss the overall impression these sources give of the events of Dunkirk.
You might want to suggest some descriptions, e.g. heroic, glorious, brave, organised, successful, a shambles, chaotic, cowardly . . . and ask which ones best sum up the impression created by these sources.

**Did you know?**

As an extra dimension to Sources 2–9, pupils should be pointed towards this information, which explains how carefully accounts at the time were controlled.

**Looking back**

**Question 1:** Sources 10–14 were all written much later than Sources 2–9. Again, they should be looked at together to see what overall impression they create. The same list of descriptions as for question 3 above could be used as a starting point.

**Questions 1–7:** These explore in various ways the reasons for the differences between the two sets of sources, and between the sources within each set. Having tackled these questions pupils ought to be in a position to realise that this is not a case of one set of sources being right and the other set being wrong. However, pupils should also explore why the sources differ. The contemporary accounts had a particular purpose and were produced in a particular context and climate of opinion. There was also limited evidence available, and that which was made available was controlled by the government. In contrast, the later accounts are based on a wider range of evidence. They have been produced for different purposes, and in a different climate and context. They do not prove the first set of accounts to be wrong, but to some extent ask different questions about Dunkirk, and come up with interpretations which supplement those we get from the first set of accounts.

With access to both sets of interpretations, we gain a much richer understanding of the event than if we had just one of them.

It is interesting to compare two different interpretations of these events by Churchill. In 1940, shortly after Dunkirk, Churchill said to Parliament and the British people, 'We must be very careful not to describe Dunkirk as a victory. Wars are not won by evacuations.' and yet, after the War, Churchill wrote, 'The tale of Dunkirk will shine in whatever records are preserved of our affairs.'

Churchill's 1940 speech sits oddly with the other accounts we have from the time and with the government's aim of keeping morale high. It may be that Churchill was afraid that the government had been too successful in creating a picture of Dunkirk as a triumph, and that he was worried people had not realised what a difficult situation they were in and what struggles lay ahead. Writing after the War, he no longer had such worries.

## ENQUIRY: THE BATTLE OF BRITAIN: A TURNING POINT?

Pupils' Book pp. 162–163

This single-spread enquiry is the first of several which concentrate on particularly significant episodes in the War.

The term 'turning point' will need to be discussed in class. It is a difficult and imprecise concept. It might be helpful to explain that turning points:
■ take place over a short period of time
■ are usually made up of just one event
■ often bring about a completely new situation.

It might help to think of turning points in pupils' lives. Gradually growing older over the years is a trend, but leaving school, leaving home, starting work and getting a whole new set of friends might be a turning point.

Returning to the Battle of Britain, it was clear that by the summer of 1940 the general trend of the War was in Germany's favour. Much of mainland Europe had been conquered. The conquest of Britain could be seen as the next stage in this trend; it would not involve any change in policy, nor would it, if successful, change the progress of the War, i.e. in Germany's favour.

However, as we all know, the main consequence of the Battle of Britain was that invasion plans were postponed. This was the first serious reverse Hitler had experienced. It also meant that Britain continued to pose a potential threat. Is this enough to make it a turning point? It could be argued that it slowed down an

existing trend, but did not immediately lead to Allied victory.

**Source 3:** You could illustrate the time given to recovery and preparation (35 minutes) by reference to your school lunch break.

**Source 4:** You (or the pupils) could make these figures into a graph to visualise the shape of the battle more clearly.

**Question 3:** Different pupils might use different criteria in judging why the British won. It is possible to base the judgement on:
■ the number of aircraft destroyed (Source 4)
■ the fact that the Germans were forced to change their tactics and turn from attacking airfields to attacking cities
■ the fact that the RAF was not destroyed
■ the fact that Germany failed to gain control of the skies
■ the fact that Hitler called off the invasion plans.

Some pupils will use a combination of these, as they are connected.

The criteria that pupils use will determine how they approach the second part of the question. But they will need to consider carefully the information on this spread. How important do they think the following factors are?
■ German fighter aircraft could stay in the air over Britain for just 30 minutes.
■ The German fighters flew close together.
■ The British fighter planes attacked the German bombers rather than the fighter aircraft.
■ British factories were producing more fighter aircraft than German factories, while more German planes were shot down.

## ENQUIRY: LIVING THROUGH THE WAR: PART TWO

Pupils' Book pp. 164–171
Worksheet 40

The story of the War now returns to the Home Front in Britain in this four-spread enquiry. This represents another change of pace. The spread on the Battle of Britain was quite dense in terms of information. This new enquiry is a more leisurely examination of what life was like. Plenty of pictorial material and first-hand accounts have been used to help pupils gradually reach an understanding of the wartime experience.

The focus is on what it was like living through the Blitz. We have attempted to question the usual picture of people coping courageously with the Blitz. This theme has been dealt with by Angus Calder in his book *The Myth of the Blitz*, where he questions the conclusions he reached in his earlier book, *The People's War*. He also writes about the creation of other 'myths', such as Dunkirk.

(Pages 164–165)

## The Blitz begins

**Question 1:** Source 1 is a reconstruction based on a conversation with a man who experienced sheltering in an Anderson Shelter at first hand as a child. Pupils could be asked what kind of evidence they think it might be based on. To judge its accuracy, a comparison with Source 7 can be made, although pupils must understand that one would not expect them to be identical.

**Source 2:** It is a good idea to read this to the class to give it its full impact.

**Activity:** The leaflet could be made up on a DTP system. There are examples of government leaflets on other subjects on pages 152 and 171.

(Pages 166–167)

## Morale

This second spread looks at the way the government attempted to present the Blitz, and create an impression of the British people living bravely through it; it does this by getting the pupils to act as a government censor.

**Activity:** Some of the sources will, we hope, be judged differently by different pupils. Source 11, for instance, might show the terror of the Blitz to some, or the heroism of the British to others.

**Sources 15 and 17** are particularly important for representing the alternative and unofficial account of the Blitz.

**Question 1:** The statement is a composite of popular impressions of the Blitz gathered by the author.

(Pages 168–169)

## Working through the Blitz

This third spread concentrates on the work that people, particularly women, did on the Home Front. As with so much of this enquiry it could be supplemented with material from your own local history or with oral history from the pupils' families.

**Question 5** should embrace more than just the sources on this page. Pupils should also consider the earlier material on evacuation (pages 152–157).

(Pages 170–171)

## 'Dad's Army'

**Questions 1–3:** To get the most out of the material about the Home Guard, show pupils part of a video of *Dad's Army*.

Questions can be asked about:
■ the impression the programme creates of the Home Guard
■ how it creates this impression
■ why the programme makers may have chosen to create this particular impression
■ how accurate this impression is, judged against the evidence on page 170.

## Rationing

**Summary question 1: Worksheet 40** can be used to support this question.

## *ENQUIRY: HITLER INVADES THE USSR: THE TURNING POINT?*

Pupils' Book pp. 172–175

We have previously looked at the Battle of Britain as a possible turning point in the War. This two-spread enquiry presents an alternative 'turning point': Hitler's decision to invade the USSR.

The first spread, in particular, focuses on the strategic importance of Hitler's decision. It is often presented as a surprise move, and as an avoidable error. But on the other hand, the invasion of the USSR does appear entirely consistent with two of Hitler's long stated aims – to defeat Communism and to obtain living space for Germans.

This enquiry should also serve to emphasise to pupils the crucial role played by the Soviet army and the Soviet people in the Second World War. The War is too often taught from a Western perspective only. However, from 1941 until 1944 the USSR took the brunt of the onslaughts of the German army. If it had collapsed the War might have been virtually over. By the Soviet resistance to the German armies a breathing space was created to allow Britain to build up its forces. To use Churchill's phrase, the Soviets 'tore the heart out of the German army', but at an enormous cost: compare the casualty figures for the USSR and other Allied countries in Source 1 on page 150. A whole generation of Soviet men was lost, and even today older Russians remember the War with profound grief and anger.

Finally, this enquiry also contributes to pupils' examination of the role of Hitler and Stalin as wartime leaders:
■ Did Hitler let his obsession with fighting Communism affect his military judgement?
■ Was the sacrifice which Stalin demanded of the Soviet people worth it? Mention can be made of the evidence now being found in Russia of mass executions of Soviet troops who attempted to desert.

(Pages 172–173)

## Operation Barbarossa

A new perspective on the USSR's position at this time comes from a document discovered (or revealed) in the USSR in 1990. This document contains plans by the USSR to attack the Germans, and was signed by General Zhukov, the Soviet Chief of Staff, just five weeks before Hitler's attack on the USSR in June 1941.

The Zhukov plan was to attack German forces in German-controlled Poland. The aim was to conquer all Polish territory, as well as East Prussia. The plan is interpreted by historians as a defensive one: the Soviet strike was to have been limited and the aim was to use Poland as a buffer against possible German aggression. There appears to have been no intention to attack Germany on a larger scale.

The plan may have resulted from information passed to Stalin in May 1941 by a Soviet spy in Tokyo that Germany was going to attack the USSR between 20 and 22 June 1941 (the attack actually took place on 22 June). Thus the Zhukov plan can be seen as a pre-emptive strike, a defensive move.

Historians are divided over whether the Zhukov plan would have worked. Some argue that the element of surprise would have been so great as to make a subsequent *Blitzkrieg* against the USSR impossible. Others argue that given the poor state of the Soviet army the strike would have failed, and could have enabled the Germans to tear the Red Army apart with fatal consequences for the USSR, Britain and the rest of the world.

**Question 3:** Pupils who have used the earlier book in this series, *Societies in Change*, will have studied Napoleon's invasion of Russia and may usefully be able to recall some of the lessons a potential invader might learn from that failed invasion.

(Pages 174–175)

### The Siege of Leningrad, 1941–44

This second spread concentrates on one episode from the war on the Eastern Front: the Siege of Leningrad. This siege led to Leningrad becoming known as the 'hero city'. The sources vividly describe what it was like.

You could start pupils off on this spread by looking at Source 9. Pupils should already have compiled a weekly diet sheet (see question 1 on page 170). This could be compared with the figures in Source 9. What could they cut down on if they had to reduce the amount they eat daily by one third? Can they plan this and still have a diet which would keep them reasonably healthy? Would they in fact be healthier if they stopped eating some of the things they regularly eat?

You could also discuss what things we could eat without any harm to ourselves which we do not normally regard as suitable as food. A list could be compiled on the board. There are opportunities for cross-curricular work with the Science department on diet.

**Activity:** Conditions in Leningrad provide other useful comparisons with life in Britain during the Blitz. For example, pupils could compare their diaries for this Activity with their diaries for Activity 2 on page 171. What are the differences and similarities?

### ENQUIRY: THE BATTLE OF THE ATLANTIC: 'THE ONLY THING THAT EVER FRIGHTENED ME'

Pupils' Book pp. 176–179
Worksheets 41, 42, 47

This two-spread enquiry introduces a third possible turning point of the War: the Battle of the Atlantic. The first focus is on why Germany lost the battle, the second on what life was like on board ship.

The quotation in the title comes from Churchill.

To introduce this spread it would be worth remembering the work on rationing on page 171, and on aircraft production during the Battle of Britain on page 162. Pupils need to appreciate how dependent Britain was on trade across the Atlantic for both food and raw materials to maintain wartime production.

(Pages 176–177)

**Source 1:** These statistics could be put onto a computer database with a graphics program.

E-boats are fast and mobile German torpedo boats.

**Question 1:** This is demanding, but with careful preparation pupils should be able to produce a detailed piece of extended writing.

It is important that pupils have practice in using and making deductions from a wide range of different types of source material. It will help if parts a) to d) are used first to organise the material.

Pupils' answers can be compared with the account provided by the authors in the second column of page 176. Ask pupils whether this account contains anything which could not be worked out from Source 1.

**Questions 2 and 3:** Each reason in Source 3 could be written on a separate card and the cards used to answer questions 2 and 3.

(Pages 177–179)

### What was life like on board ship?

**Question 1:** Your pupils may be surprised at the way the complaints seem almost trivial – more to do with food than the dangers of battle. However, this is in many ways consistent with experiences of other theatres of war: many of the complaints of soldiers in the trenches during the First World War were to do with food! Is this because it is an easier thing to complain about than danger of death?

**Source 9:** The various pictorial sources give very different impressions of the battle. How far do pupils think Source 9 is based on research and how far on imagination? What do they think the painting was for – a textbook, a novel, or something else?

**Source 11:** Pupils could be asked whether they think Source 11 comes from a diary, a memoir or a novel. The book is published in paperback by Fontana. It was first published in Germany in 1973, and in English in 1974.

In a similar vein, **Worksheet 42** (two pages), is an exercise interrogating an adventure comic version of the Land War. For question 1 the missing words are: 'Okay, Bill, it's your show,' and 'Here we go! Keep your head well down when we hit.'

**Question 6: Worksheet 47** deals with the general question of war crimes. In this context the aim of question 6 is simply to raise the issue. It is probably best used in class discussion. However, make sure pupils know what the phrase war crimes means. It is in the glossary on page 214 of the Pupils' Book, and Worksheet 47 will be useful here as background.

**Activity:** This map is on **Worksheet 41**.

## ENQUIRY: WHY DID THE JAPANESE ATTACK PEARL HARBOR?

Pupils' Book pp. 180–181

This single-spread enquiry picks up the story of events in East Asia where the enquiry *The rise of Japan* left off, and it will be helpful to refer pupils back to their work on pages 146–147.

This spread focuses on the reasons for the attack on Pearl Harbor. Pupils are told in a straightforward way the story of American–Japanese relations in the months before the attack.

### The countdown to war

You could draw these entries onto a timeline to get a better sense of the gathering pace.

### Causes and consequences

You might like to make pupils aware of the recent 'discovery' about the attack on Pearl Harbor. *The Guardian* reported in December 1992 under the headline 'Pearl Harbour "Could have been avoided" ' that an unpublished report by Sir Robert Craigie, Britain's Ambassador in Tokyo at the time, had just been discovered by his son.

The report says that the attack on Pearl Harbor was not inevitable and could have been avoided by negotiation. Winston Churchill was so angered by this report that he ordered it should be destroyed. However, it seems that one copy of the report survived. Churchill later wrote, 'It was a blessing that Japan attacked the United States and thus brought America wholeheartedly into the War.' After the attack and America's declaration of war, Churchill said, 'So we have won the War after all. As for the Japanese, they will be ground to powder.'

It is also now being claimed that Churchill had information about the impending attack on Pearl Harbor, but kept it from the Americans; it seems that British and Commonwealth agents had been breaking the Japanese naval code for years.

**Activity:** Each possible cause could be put onto a separate card for pupils to use for answering questions 1–3.

## ENQUIRY: EXPERIENCES OF WAR

Pupils' Book pp. 182–185

This two-spread enquiry covers areas of the War not included in other enquiries. The emphasis is very much on people's experiences. It bears comparison with experiences of people on the Home Front in Britain.

The areas covered are Japanese internees in the USA, civilians and soldiers in Russia and the Ukraine, the desert war in North Africa, soldiers and prisoners of war in South-East Asia, and the experiences of people in China.

**Source 1:** You could make a large version of this map to display at the front of the class, adding to it other coloured dots to show the locations of the case studies in earlier enquiries. It will help to give the picture of this war as truly a 'world war'. It could be contrasted with the rather more limited theatres of war of the First World War.

Pupils could be split into groups to work on one of the following case studies each.

(Pages 182–183)

### Case study 1: Japanese Americans

**Question 1:** The different treatment of the Japanese and the Germans is one aspect of this question. It emphasises among other things the point made in the previous enquiry (page 180) that the Americans were more concerned about the war in the Pacific than the war in Europe. It also raises questions of racism in that many more Americans, and many more powerful Americans, were of Germanic descent than Japanese descent.

### Case study 2: Russia and the Ukraine

**Question 1:** This is designed to get pupils to consider the dehumanising effects of war.

(Pages 183–184)

### Case study 3: The North African desert

You might want to preface this case study by explaining how the British and Germans came to be fighting in the North African desert.

(Pages 184–185)

### Case study 4: South-East Asia

**Question 1:** Source 14 shows the medical section of a PoW camp. Pupils might see this as a sign that prisoners were well cared for. However, the hardships of life in South-East Asia were such that 7500 British prisoners died of disease.

### Case study 5: China

If pupils are working in groups on separate case studies, get the group working on China to compare, for example, how Sources 16 and 17 compare with Sources 5–7 on the treatment of civilians in the USSR.

**Question 1:** If pupils have been working separately on different case studies, this question can be treated as part of the reporting back process, with each group or individual contributing details of their case study to the lists of hardships and sufferings of soldiers and civilians.

## ENQUIRY: HOW DID THE HOLOCAUST HAPPEN?

Pupils' Book pp. 186–193
Worksheets 43, 47

This four-spread enquiry tackles the difficult subject of the Holocaust.

A careful attempt has been made to:
- set the Holocaust in its historical context (pages 186–187)
- explain how the German people were propagandised (pages 186–188)
- avoid presenting the Jews as passive victims by using a series of case studies of various forms of Jewish resistance (pages 192–193)
- show the dehumanising effect of being actively involved in the Final Solution (pages 189–192)
- avoid dehumanising the millions of Jews who died.

The enquiry takes pupils through the different stages in the persecution of the Jews, from discrimination to concentration camps, to the ghettos, to the 'Final Solution'. One question to emerge from this is whether the 'Final Solution' was planned by Hitler from the beginning (given his ideas and attitudes in the 1920s and early 1930s), or whether he had no idea where his initial ideas would take him.

Sources 7, 13, 14, 19, 21 and 22 are sufficiently disturbing to need careful handling in class. You might want to use these only selectively; certainly you should prepare pupils in advance. However gruesome, events in history should be confronted. It was the inability of people to believe that anything as terrible as the Holocaust could ever take place that in many ways allowed it to happen.

Attempts should also be made to make links with the world today, e.g. 'ethnic cleansing' in what was Yugoslavia.

Further materials which might be useful include:
- *Through our Eyes: Children Witness the Holocaust* by Itzhak Tatelbaum (textbook and video looking at children's experiences through diaries, poems, photographs and drawings)
- *The War Against the Jews* by David Altshuler (deals with different themes and moral issues related to the Holocaust).

(Pages 190–191)

### The 'Final Solution'

**Question 1:** Pupils may find it helpful to look again at their answers to question 3 on page 187 and question 2 on page 188 and to think about whether there is evidence in the earlier sources that the 'Final Solution' was planned all along.

(Pages 192–193)

**Question 3: Worksheet 47** deals with the subject of war crimes. It should ideally be used after the enquiry on Hiroshima (pages 198–201), when a number of possible war crimes have been studied. However, question 1 can be used here.

### Jewish resistance

Since the first edition of this book, the highly successful film *Schindler's List* has highlighted one example of a German who helped the Jews – as well as dramatically illustrating the human tragedy of the Holocaust.

**Source 30** comes from *An Artist's Journal of the Holocaust* by Alfred Kantor, published in 1987 by Judy Piatkus.

**Activity:** Pupils may need a good deal of support in this exercise. They obviously cannot consider all of Sources 1–31, so you could point them towards three or four – e.g. Source 21 for Hitler's obsession, which helps pupils reflect on whether the situation for the Jews could ever improve while Hitler was still in charge, Source 11 for the life they might expect outside the camp, Source 19 for the life (or rather, death) they can expect if they stay in the camp, Source 27 and the text above it for possible tactics of resistance, the text beneath Source 29 for the possibility of resistance in the camp.

Ideally, they should work in groups of four and each person should list the advantages and disadvantages of one of the possible courses of action.

**Worksheet 43,** which has two pages, allows international reaction to the persecution and mass murder of Jews to be studied in more detail. It should be used as an extension sheet for more able pupils.

## ENQUIRY: SHOULD DRESDEN HAVE BEEN BOMBED?

Pupils' Book pp. 194–197
Worksheets 44, 47

This two-spread enquiry is important, as it shows that German civilians suffered just as badly, if not worse, than British civilians during the War. It also turns the moral spotlight on Allied policy for a change.

You may wish to start by brainstorming the idea of war crimes, so as to see what pupils already know.

There will be some pupils who will be able to give examples either from their general knowledge of previous wars or from whatever conflict is in the news at the time. Some will mention the events we have already studied in this context: the Holocaust and the U-boat campaign.

Tease out a discussion as to whether some things are 'acceptable' and others 'unacceptable' in wartime, or does 'anything go'?

The advantage of considering this before looking at the Dresden material is that pupils can set up hypotheses about what constitutes a war crime, which can then be tested in the Dresden case study.

**Worksheet 47** turns the spotlight on Allied leaders, including Churchill and Sir Arthur Harris, but is best tackled after the Hiroshima enquiry.

The first spread of this enquiry takes a brief look at how ideas about bombing gradually changed during the twentieth century, and at the decision to bomb German cities during the Second World War.

Most historians would not question the legitimacy of bombing German cities during the War. However, the bombing of Dresden does raise different and difficult issues: the War was nearing its end, the German army was in full retreat, the residential areas would appear to have been deliberately targeted (see Source 11), and at the time Dresden was full of refugees who were flocking into the city in their thousands. This enquiry aims to explore whether the bombing of Dresden was different from earlier bombing.

(Pages 194–195)

### Changing ideas about bombing

**Source 3** shows the 'acceptable' face of bombing – the low flying bomber delivering an accurate hit on what we take to be a dockside factory or warehouse. The question of precision bombing is relevant, as it is returned to later. Reference could be made to precision bombing in recent conflicts, such as the Gulf War.

### Reactions to the bombing

From their work on the Blitz pupils will probably be able to understand the natural anxiety of the British people that raids on Germany would lead to reprisal raids on British cities.

### Bomber Harris

Reference could be made to the statue of 'Bomber' Harris (Sir Arthur Harris) erected in the Strand, London, in May 1992. The statue was unveiled by the Queen Mother at a ceremony attended by several hundred bomber crew veterans who raised £100,000 for the making of the statue. They believed that Fighter Command (through events like the Battle of Britain) had captured all the glory.

Since then the statue has been regularly attacked by peace protestors, who have sprayed red paint over it and daubed the word 'shame' across it.

The statue has also caused controversy in Dresden. When the Queen visited the city in September 1992 there was a demonstration and eggs were thrown at the Queen. To quote *The Times* of 20 October 1992 (alongside a vivid photograph of the statue sprayed with red paint), 'Opponents of Bomber Harris view him as a mass murderer, but others believe his strategy of reducing major German centres of population and industry to rubble and submission helped to shorten the war by several months.'

(Pages 196–197)

### Was the bombing justified?

**Source 12:** This defends the Allies' strategy, and as it is the only source that does so directly you need to make sure pupils have read and understood it.

**Sources 13 and 15** raise again the issue of precision bombing.

**Summary question 2** raises some important points about the morality of certain actions during a war. It will be best to discuss each bulleted point in class first.

**Worksheet 44** can be used to focus on the question of why writers disagree about the Dresden bombing. It provides a framework of reasons why historians disagree, and interpret the past in different ways. It has been adapted from Arthur Marwick's Open University framework. Pupils can add extra reasons where appropriate and the framework can be adapted to any debate, e.g. those on Dunkirk, the Blitz or Hiroshima.

### ENQUIRY: WAS THE DROPPING OF THE ATOMIC BOMBS JUSTIFIED?

Pupils' Book pp. 198–201
Worksheets 45, 46, 47

This two-spread enquiry investigates the last big question of the Second World War. The effects of the bombs are given on the first spread, but the main focus is the motives behind their use, and whether it was justified.

(Pages 198–199)

### Victory in Europe

This information is necessary to give the pupils some overall context for the events in Japan. We have kept it short and to the point, although you may, of course, want to make a lot more of this.

The story of D-Day, the advance on Berlin, and the death of Hitler can make for a vivid narrative. Source 4 on page 151 will provide a background for telling this story.

This period is also summarised again in the story strip on page 208.

**Worksheet 45** will help pupils to complete their overall picture of the war in Europe. It provides a sequencing exercise (at two levels of difficulty) on events of the war in Europe, with an additional element focusing on reasons for the Allies' success. It can be used at the end of this spread.

Ask pupils to cut up the page and mount the events onto card. If pupils work in groups you do not need one card per pupil. The first page of the worksheet is for all pupils, the second page for more able pupils.

Questions 1 and 5 must in both cases be done without resort to books, to see if pupils can sequence by the logic of events. You may well want to go over their answers with them as a class by building up the correct sequence on the board.

Pupils should be allowed to use the textbook and other reference books for the rest of the questions.

The sequence is:

Germany and USSR sign Nazi–Soviet Pact (August 1939)
Germany invades Poland (1 September 1939)
Britain and France declare war on Germany (3 September 1939)
Churchill replaces Chamberlain as Prime Minister (May 1940)
Germany conquers Belgium (28 May 1940)
British and Allied troops evacuated from Dunkirk (end May–early June 1940)
Germans take Paris (14 June 1940)
Battle of Britain won by RAF (17 September 1940)
Germany invades USSR (June 1941)
Germany declares war on USA (11 December 1941)
Germans surrender at Stalingrad (2 February 1943)
Allies land in Sicily (June 1943)
D-Day landings (6 June 1944)
USSR invades Romania (20 August 1944)
Allies take Paris (25 August 1944)
Soviet army reaches Berlin (April 1945)
Hitler commits suicide (30 April 1945)
German army surrenders (8 May 1945)

### Victory in Japan

Pupils should understand the distinction between different types of nuclear bombs. There are three types: the atom bomb, the hydrogen bomb and the thermonuclear bomb.

■ The atom bomb (used at Hiroshima and Nagasaki) explodes from the fission or breaking up of uranium or plutonium.

■ The hydrogen bomb can achieve a much larger explosion – the fission explosion is used to set off a fusion of hydrogen atoms, resulting in an enormous release of energy.

■ The themonuclear bomb produces the largest explosion. The fusion bomb is blanketed by stable uranium – this helps create a further larger fission explosion.

By today's standards the Hiroshima bomb was small, although it exploded with a power 2000 times greater than the heaviest Blitz bombing of London. The modern Minuteman missile carries 335-kiloton warheads, each 25 times bigger than the Hiroshima bomb.

**Question 2:** A particularly useful comparison will be between Source 2 and Source 8 on page 196.

### Why did they drop the bombs?

**Question 1:** Pupils are given reasons which have been suggested for the dropping of the two bombs. The class could discuss these. Judgements reached here can be returned to in the Activity on page 201.

(Pages 200–201)

**Sources 8–20:** The material on the second spread could be made more accessible by pointing pupils to the following sources, which provide evidence for or against each point:

■ to save the lives of American troops (For: Sources 8, 9, 13, 14. Against: Sources 10, 11, 12)
■ to try out a bomb on which so much money had been spent (For: Sources 15, 16 and 20. Against: Source 18)
■ to impress the Soviets (Source 17)
■ to teach Japan a lesson (Source 19).

The alternative is to give pupils a list of reasons for dropping the bomb, as in the diagram opposite. This includes much of the information in Sources 8–20 and some more as well.

Pupils can display these reasons on a spider diagram like the one below, adding connections between reasons if they can see them. They can then move on to **Worksheet 46,** which provides a grid for analysing the evidence in Sources 8–20.

At the end of this section you might like to return to question 1 on page 150 of the Pupils' Book and reconsider pupils' positioning of the headings. If you do so, use **Worksheet 45.**

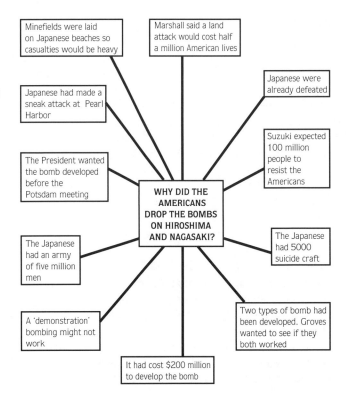

**Worksheet 47:** This looks at the broad question of war crimes: what they are and how they should be punished.

# Section 4: The role of wartime leaders

## ENQUIRY: CHURCHILL AND HITLER AS WAR LEADERS

Pupils' Book pp. 202–205

This two-spread enquiry compares Churchill and Hitler as wartime leaders. The first spread examines how both men were presented to the public by their own governments and the media. The second spread compares these official images with other evidence about them.

(With thanks to Peter Mantin for ideas and material.)

(Pages 202–203)

**Questions 1–4:** This introductory material is best dealt with through class or group discussion.

Encourage pupils to distinguish between peacetime leadership and war leadership. Many historians agree that Churchill's qualities were not suited to peacetime leadership.

## Churchill: the public image

**Questions 1–2:** These are intended for class discussion.

## Hitler: the public image

**Questions 3–4:** These are also intended for class discussion.

**Question 5:** Pupils should write their answers down so that they can be re-examined after all the evidence on the following spread has been used, and in particular when they answer question 3 on page 205.

**Activity:** This is clearly a major task and much written work can be generated. One advantage of this task is that it will reveal not only pupils' understanding of the material on this spread, but also their grasp of a much wider set of issues tackled throughout this unit.

(Pages 204–205)

## Churchill and Hitler: the reality

**Sources 10–16:** Pupils could also be made aware of the recent revisionist view of Churchill's wartime leadership. If presented simply this could lead to useful class discussion.

The revisionist view is to be found most fully in John Charmley's *Churchill: The End of Glory*. However, a popular and less subtle version has been put forward by

Alan Clark. The summary given below is based on Clark's views.

Clark criticises Churchill's decision that once arms were taken up against Germany they should not be laid down until Germany was totally defeated. He argues that by fighting until Germany was defeated Churchill exhausted Britain. This meant it was finished as a world power and that its Empire was bound to be lost.

He goes on to argue that Churchill liquidated Britain's enormous overseas investments to pay for American supplies so that the War could be prolonged and Germany finally defeated.

He argues that there were several occasions when beneficial terms could, and should, have been reached with Mussolini and Hitler.

The first opportunity (although Clark is not clear about whether this was the right time for a deal) was in May 1940. France had almost fallen, Italy was poised to attack, the situation looked grim and an invasion of Britain by Germany looked imminent. The Cabinet discussed a peace plan suggested by Halifax. The plan was:

■ to offer Mussolini Gibraltar, Malta, the French colonies or Corsica, or a protectorate over Egypt
■ to ask Mussolini to mediate with Hitler. Hitler could be offered the return of the German colonies. The new frontiers in Europe (i.e. Germany's recent conquests) would be recognised. Governments (of conquered countries) in exile in London would be banished.

Clark argues that there were other occasions when a peace could have been struck. For example:
■ In July 1940, before the Battle of Britain, Hitler offered peace terms. These were still on offer even after the Battle of Britain.
■ In spring 1941, following the defeat of the Italians in Africa, Hitler wanted to secure his western flank before he turned on the USSR. He sent his deputy, Hess, to Britain with terms. Churchill refused to see Hess and suppressed the documents. (Churchill is reported to have said 'Well, even if it is Hess, I am going to watch the Marx Brothers.') Clark argues that if peace had been made then, the British fleet and the Spitfires could have been moved to Singapore. The Japanese would never have attacked and the British Empire in the East would have been saved.

Clark goes on to argue that since Churchill was obsessed with defeating Hitler, he had to bring the USA into the War, and this meant allowing a Japanese attack (see page 88 of this book).

Clark concludes, 'The war went on far too long, and when Britain emerged the country was bust. Nothing remained of assets overseas. Without immense and punitive borrowings from the US we would have starved. The Empire was terminally damaged.'

Other historians have replied by arguing that Hitler simply could not be trusted. How much, given Hitler's earlier track record on keeping promises, would any negotiated peace with Hitler have been worth? If Britain had let Hitler take the USSR he would have dominated all of Europe, and sooner or later he would inevitably have threatened Britain.

They also question how serious Hitler's so-called peace offers were. For example, it is not at all clear that Hess came to Britain with Hitler's permission or was carrying Hitler's plans.

There is also the moral argument that Hitler was evil and that Britain could not leave millions of people to suffer under permanent Nazi rule.

Pupils could be asked whether Churchill was right to fight on until Germany was defeated, or whether an early peace would have been justified if British independence could have been guaranteed.

**Sources 17–22:** Here are some other recent historians' judgements on Hitler which could be used to supplement those in the Pupils' Book.

> *It is certainly true that Hitler's unorthodox and risky plans were at times more effective than the conventional attitudes of the commanders. But Hitler made the mistake of taking a few successes as a sign of his absolute military genius. He often pointed out to them that Germany would never have achieved anything if they had been in charge.*

> *He could not tolerate anything that smacked of criticism and would often answer even the politest objection with utter silence or with the dismissal of the conference.*

> *[On his Soviet policy] His refusal to admit his mistakes and benefit from experience led to a further chain of catastrophes for the troops. Hitler kept to a policy of no retreat long after it was clear his Russian policy was doomed.*

**Extension exercise:** If there is time, pupils should choose one contemporary leader and collect different images and judgements of that leader in the press today.

## ENQUIRY: STALIN AND ROOSEVELT: FRIENDS OR ENEMIES?

Pupils' Book pp. 206–207

This single spread compares Stalin and Roosevelt in a rather different way to how Churchill and Hitler were compared.

Most of the text is devoted to a comparison of the backgrounds of the two men. There are some interesting similarities as well as more obvious differences.

**Question 3:** Pupils should be directed to the written sources – Sources 2, 3, 5, 6 and 8.

# Section 5: Conclusion

## ENQUIRY: A BETTER WORLD?

Pupils' Book pp. 208–213
Worksheets 45, 48

This final three-spread enquiry provides an overview of the legacy of the Second World War for Britain, Europe and the world. This could be an immense topic, so we have strictly limited ourselves to the breakdown of the relationship between the Allies (pages 208–210), refugees (page 211) and the UN and the Universal Declaration of Human Rights (pages 212–213).

(Pages 208–209)

### The Allies fall out
**Worksheet 45** allows pupils to piece together their picture of the War as a whole. It is ideally used on page 198 or 199, but could be used here instead.

The unfolding of the negotiations towards the end and after the end of the War is a complicated topic. The comic strip format has been used to tell this story as clearly as possible.

The two main conferences, Yalta and Potsdam, and the differences which gradually emerged during these conferences, provide the focus, which is then picked up by question 1 over the page.

(Pages 210–211)

### Soviet attitudes/Western attitudes
**Source 3** comes from a satirical Soviet magazine, *Krokodil*, of 1948 (we have replaced the original Russian captions with English translations). An 'Uncle Sam' figure, representing the USA with his stars and stripes shirt and trousers, is talking to a Soviet peasant, shipbuilder, banker and politician. Clearly the perceived objective of the Marshall Plan is the undermining of Soviet industry and commerce and of Soviet political sovereignty.

**Source 6** was published in the *Evening Standard*, 2 March 1948. Stalin sits at his desk, facing a photo of the US Secretary of State Marshall (of Marshall Aid fame). The downward-pointing switches are countries which, in the cartoonist's view, were already under the sway of Communism. The caption reminds us that both the USA and the USSR spoke of their own system as 'freedom'.

### The refugees
**Worksheet 48:** This allows pupils to summarise the territorial changes in Europe from 1914 to 1919 and 1945.

(Pages 212–213)

## The United Nations

**Source 12** appeared in the *Manchester Guardian* on 30 June 1950. The United Nations, hand in hand with the USA, is armed and ready to act. It is a more dynamic force than the League, now consigned to its grave, but shown holding up its hands in horror. The caption suggests that the lessons of history have been learned.

**Source 13A** shows Roosevelt, Stalin and Churchill going into the 'Votes and Vetoes' show. The small nations are not allowed in. This is a comment on the voting procedure of the UN Security Council, and the special privileges of the three big powers.

**Source 13B** was published on 4 June 1945. Stalin, Churchill, Truman and De Gaulle are lining up outside the UN club, but each is preparing for a different game. The cartoonist is commenting on the problems faced by the United Nations, with each country having its own objectives.

There will doubtless be a current crisis area where the UN is monitoring affairs or deploying peace-keeping forces at the time you use this unit.

According to *The Guardian* in January 1993, the UN has 52,000 military personnel (and many more civilians) working in twelve trouble spots around the world. They are (with date of commencement of activity and examples of work done):

■ Former Yugoslavia (since 1992): keeping airport open for relief work and repairing electricity and water supplies.

■ El Salvador (since 1991): monitoring human rights and trying to settle civil war.

■ Somalia (since 1992): negotiating cease-fires and delivering food aid.

■ Western Sahara (since 1991): helping prepare and run a referendum on the future of the area.

■ Angola (since 1989): monitoring withdrawal of Cuban troops and the conduct of elections.

■ Mozambique (since 1993): monitoring peace deal to end civil war.

■ Cambodia (since 1992): overseeing elections and monitoring cease-fire.

■ Kashmir (since 1949): monitoring cease-fire line between India and Pakistan.

■ Kuwait (since 1991): patrolling the cease-fire zone between Kuwait and Iraq following the Gulf War.

■ Cyprus (since 1964): preventing recurrence of Greek–Turkish War.

■ Lebanon (since 1978): overseeing withdrawal of Israel from Southern Lebanon and helping Lebanese government reassert authority.

■ Golan Heights (since 1974): monitoring buffer zone between Syria and Israel.

■ Israel (since 1948): monitoring affairs in Israel.

**Question 2:** Pupils could also discuss whether any important rights have been left out.

## The legacy of the Second World War

We have kept our coverage of the post-war period brief.

For many people this unit – The Twentieth-Century World – will be used at the end of a Y9 course. Whether to, and how to, further develop their overview and/or depth studies of the post-war period will be determined by many factors: are pupils going on to GCSE? If they are, which syllabus? If they are not, then how can their experience of compulsory History be brought to a successful, worthwhile and motivating conclusion? However you choose to focus your work on the post-war period, it is important to take into account the particular needs of your pupils and their ongoing education.

A rapid overview of vast and complex topics such as the Cold War is unlikely to meet many people's requirements. On the other hand a depth study of selected aspects of post-war life might: examples are the changing role of women; changes in popular culture – looking at music, television, sport, etc.; a case study of decolonisation; the development of multi-cultural Britain.

More advice on different approaches will be offered in our forthcoming Special Needs Support Materials for this unit.

# Causes of the First World War

1. In the table below write down any evidence you can find on pages 110–113 of your textbook for any of the six countries doing something to bring war closer. You can see that a few entries have been made already.
2. When you have completed the table, decide on the score out of ten you are going to give to each country. This score will not just depend on the number of entries you have made for each country. Some of the entries will be of little importance, while others will be very important. You need to judge the entries for each country.

|  | Responsible for causing the War in the long term | Responsible for triggering off the War |
|---|---|---|
| Britain | starts building Dreadnoughts | declares war on Germany |
| Germany | colonial ambitions | invades Belgium |
| France | agrees to Triple Entente to surround Germany | |
| Austria | | attacks Serbia |
| Serbia | | assassination of the Archduke |
| Russia | | |

# Peacemaking at Versailles

IN THIS exercise you are faced with the same decisions as the peacemakers at Versailles. How would you have dealt with the problems facing Europe in 1919?

## INSTRUCTIONS

1. Work in groups of four. Each of you should take on the role of either President Wilson of the USA, Lloyd George (the British Prime Minister), Clemenceau (the French Prime Minister), or the head of the German delegation, Count Brockdorff-Rantzau. Study the ideas of the 'Big Three' leaders and the German viewpoint on this page.

2. First you should decide whether Germany should be allowed to discuss the terms of the Treaty. But only Wilson, Lloyd George and Clemenceau actually take part in this decision. If you decide NO, then the person playing Count Brockdorff-Rantzau must sit in silence for the rest of the debate, but should write down their opinions and feelings on each decision.

3. Then each group should attempt one set of problems:
   ■ 'Punishment' (Problems 1–4) or
   ■ 'Germany's eastern border' (Problems 5–8) or
   ■ 'Germany's western border' (Problems 9–13).
   For each of the problems try to agree on one of the choices, or on an alternative of your own – take a vote if necessary. Remember to look at these problems from the point of view of the country and person you are representing.

Your teacher will decide which group tackles which set of problems. Your teacher will also set a time limit, as these problems need to be dealt with as quickly as possible.

4. ■ For Problems 1–4 tick the appropriate box.
   ■ For Problems 5–8 and 9–13 colour the problem areas on Source 1 in the colour code for your decision. For example, if you decide on decision b) for Problem 6, colour the area marked 6 red.

When each group has finished, or time is up:

5. President Wilson should report the group's decisions to the class.

6. Draw up one final Treaty for the whole class.

7. Back in your groups, ask the person playing Count Brockdorff-Rantzau what they think of each term of the Treaty.

8. Each of you should write a report to your country's government on how satisfied you are with the terms of the final class Treaty.

9. Compare your group's decisions with the actual decisions on pages 116–117 of your textbook. What similarities and differences are there? Have you dealt with Germany more harshly than the peacemakers at Versailles did?

## THE AIMS

### The USA
The USA had suffered a great deal less than Europe in the War. Wilson believed that punishing Germany would only make Germany want revenge. This would mean more trouble in the future. Wilson suggested Fourteen Points which he felt would bring world peace. He wanted countries such as Poland and Czechoslovakia, which were neighbours of Germany, to become strong and independent. He wanted France to feel safe against another German attack. And he wanted to set up a League of Nations – an organisation to protect world peace.

### France
Much of the War had taken place in France. The damage to France was staggering: 75,000 homes and 23,000 factories had been destroyed. One and a half million young French men had died. Clemenceau wanted to punish Germany for this, and he wanted compensation as well. He also wanted to make sure France was safe from another attack.

### Britain
Lloyd George wanted to make a fair settlement. He agreed with many of Wilson's Fourteen Points. But the British public were demanding that Germany be harshly punished.

### Germany
The Germans did not believe the War was their fault. But they now feared that because they had lost the War they would be the ones to be punished. Politicians in Germany who wanted to set up a democratic government were worried that this might be more difficult if Germany was dealt with too harshly. However, they knew they would have to accept whatever terms the 'Big Three' decided.

*continued* ▶

# WORSHEET 28

▶ continued

## THE PROBLEMS

Your group should work on one of these three sets of problems: 'Punishment' (Problems 1–4), 'Germany's eastern border' (Problems 5–8), 'Germany's western border' (Problems 9–13).

Problems 5–13 all concern areas of land on Germany's borders, some of which are claimed by other countries. You must decide what should happen to these areas. See Source 1.

---

### PUNISHMENT

**1** Who was to blame for causing the War?
a) Germany ☐
b) other countries ☐
c) no country in particular. ☐

**2** Should Germany pay reparations for war damage?
a) Germany should not be made to pay reparations. ☐
b) Yes, a small amount – £100,000,000. ☐
c) Yes, a medium amount – £2,000,000,000. ☐
d) Yes, a large amount – £6,600,000,000. ☐

**3** Will you limit Germany's armed forces?
a) Germany's armed forces should not be limited. ☐
b) Germany should have no armed forces. ☐
c) Germany should have a small number of men and weapons. ☐
d) Germany should have equal numbers to France. ☐

**4** Will you allow Germany to keep its colonies (overseas territories)? Germany believes they are very important to help its trade and industry to recover.
a) Yes ☐
b) No ☐
c) Yes, some of them. ☐

---

### GERMANY'S EASTERN BORDER

**5** Austria–Hungary was split up. Austria is a German-speaking country which may want to unite with Germany. Should you forbid this?
a) Yes (red)
b) No (blue)
c) Yes, for fifteen years, then let the people of Austria decide (green).

**6** Who should control the important German trading port of Danzig, which is claimed by Poland?
a) Germany (blue)
b) Poland (red)
c) International control (League of Nations) (green).

**7** What should happen to the areas of West Prussia and Posen? Most of the people are German but Poland needs these areas for access to the Baltic Sea.
a) Give them to Germany (blue)
b) Give them to Poland (red)
c) International control (League of Nations) (green).

**8** Who should control the Sudetenland (part of the old Austro–Hungarian Empire)? Its people are mostly German, but it has mountains which would make Czechoslovakia easier to defend against German attack.
a) Germany (blue)
b) Czechoslovakia (red)
c) Let the Sudetenland govern itself (green).

continued ▶

▶ continued

---

## GERMANY'S WESTERN BORDER

**9** Who should control Alsace–Lorraine? Germany took this important industrial area from France in 1870. The population is mixed, but is more French than German.
a) Germany (blue)
b) France (red)
c) Put Alsace–Lorraine under international control (League of Nations) (green).

**10** Should France be given the important German coalmining area, the Saar?
a) No, let Germany keep it (blue)
b) Yes, give it to France (red)
c) Put it under international control (League of Nations) for fifteen years, then let the population decide (green).

**11** Should Belgium be given the German area of Eupen–Malmédy to help pay for the damage done to Belgium by Germany?

a) No, let Germany keep it (blue)
b) Yes, give it to Belgium (red)
c) Create a new independent state (green).

**12** Who should control the Rhineland? The people are German, but France wants it separated from Germany to make it more difficult for Germany to attack France again.
a) Germany (blue)
b) Germany, but no weapons or soldiers allowed there (blue and white stripes)
c) France (red)
d) Make it a new independent country (green).

**13** Should Denmark be given all or part of Schleswig, which has mostly Germans in the south and Danes in the north?
a) No, let Germany keep it (blue)
b) Yes, give it to Denmark (red)
c) Give them half each (blue and red stripes).

---

## SOURCE 1

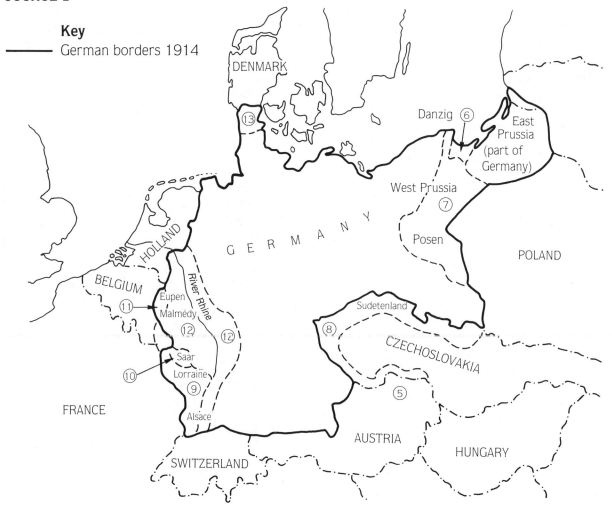

**Key**
——— German borders 1914

# **W**hy support Hitler?

IT IS sometimes difficult to understand why anyone in Germany gave their support to Hitler. The following source should help you to understand. It comes from a book called *The Past is Myself* by Christabel Bielenberg, published in 1968. Christabel, who was British but was married to a German lawyer, lived in Germany during the 1930s. Both she and her husband opposed the Nazis. Here she recalls a conversation she had in 1939 with her gardener Herr Neisse.

Work in pairs.
1. What evidence is there in Source 1 that Herr Neisse supported Hitler?
2. What reasons does he give for supporting Hitler?
3. Continue the conversation between Christabel and Herr Neisse. Christabel has to try and persuade Herr Neisse that he should not support Hitler, while Herr Neisse must argue that Hitler has been good for Germany. You will find the information on pages 118–121 of your textbook about Germany between 1919 and 1945 helpful.

### SOURCE 1

"Herr Neisse was the son of a Saxon peasant. He had fought in the Great War and returned to the chaos of Berlin a little surprised at the sudden complete German defeat. 'You see we were told of great victories, we seemed to be doing all right and then suddenly finish, the government sued for peace. I came back to Berlin to my Hilde.'

She must have been a great girl because she waited ten years before Herr Neisse collected enough funds to marry her. He tried everything to get a job as a gardener, walking from house to house. He did not drink, or smoke, worked for his lunch and starved for the rest of the day . . . but both he and Hilde managed to save.

Herr Neisse had not known quite who had been to blame for Germany losing the War, but there was no doubt in his mind that what happened in 1923 was the result of a terrible plot.

In the disastrous months of 1923 his savings, Hilde's savings, their hopes, all vanished overnight. 'The inflation, you see . . . suddenly we had nothing. With my savings I was able to buy one cup and one saucer. Funny, wasn't it?'

Not funny really, because his voice shook as he spoke . . . The loss of his little bank account shattered whatever faith he had in the Weimar Republic [the government up to 1933] and his own self respect.

Unemployment had followed as many of the middle-class people in the town had also been ruined. When their houses were taken over by Jews and shopkeepers, he eventually went to work for them. Slowly, with the aid of Hilde, he watched his little allotment grow and for two years they had enough to live on. Aged nearly 40 they at last married . . .

Then came 1929 and a huge wave rolled over Europe and America, leaving a trail of bankruptcies and suicides behind. The Neisses lost the chance to own half a vegetable stall and he lost his job.

He joined an army of six million unemployed and, although they did not actually starve because of the allotment, they were back to where they started . . .

Communism did not appeal to him; he had always worked for the better off and didn't want to bust the whole thing up, he just wanted to belong somewhere. National Socialism was more like it. He began to go to Party meetings . . . he was told that the Jews were the evil root of all Germany's ills.

'Oh no, you must not get me wrong, not one particular Jew . . . No, no. International Jewry.'

A party member by 1931, he knew of the corruption of party members, but he believed Hitler knew nothing of it. 'He is a child lover; he loves dogs too.'"

# **H**ow are dictatorships and democracies different?

THIS chart will help you to organise your research for question 1 on page 123 of your textbook. When you are filling in the columns for the USSR, Italy and Germany, try to give examples. Don't worry if you cannot fill every column for every question.

|  | Dictatorships | | | Democracies |
|---|---|---|---|---|
|  | USSR | Italy | Germany |  |
| How does the government come to power? |  |  |  |  |
| What methods does the government use to stay in power? |  |  |  |  |
| How important is the leader of the government? |  |  |  |  |
| How are political opponents treated? |  |  |  |  |
| Tick which of these freedoms people have: ■ to hold the religious beliefs they want to ■ to belong to a trade union ■ to criticise the government ■ to go on strike |  |  |  |  |
| How are the press and radio treated? |  |  |  |  |

*continued* ▶

# WORKSHEET 30

〜〜〜〜〜〜〜〜〜〜〜〜〜〜〜〜〜〜〜〜〜〜〜〜〜〜〜〜〜〜〜〜

▶ continued

|  | Dictatorships | | | Democracies |
|---|---|---|---|---|
|  | USSR | Italy | Germany |  |
| How is industry owned and controlled? |  |  |  |  |
| Does the government use the educational system to make children support it? |  |  |  |  |
| Are men and women treated differently, e.g. in education and jobs? |  |  |  |  |
| Are racial minorities discriminated against? |  |  |  |  |
| Can you find any other important differences between dictatorships and democracies? |  |  |  |  |

**1.** Which country would you rather have lived in during the 1920s and 1930s, the USSR, Italy or Germany? Give your reasons here.

# Do the dictators threaten peace in Europe?

| | Background information, e.g. when came to power | Beliefs/ aims/methods | What evidence is there that he wants to conquer other countries? | Is he powerful enough to be a threat to peace in Europe? | How likely is he to combine with either or both of the other two to conquer other countries? |
|---|---|---|---|---|---|
| Hitler | | | | | |
| Mussolini | | | | | |
| Stalin | | | | | |

**PEACE & WAR** THE TWENTIETH-CENTURY WORLD

# Dictatorship versus democracy in Spain

IN THE 1920s Spain was a backward country. Most of the people were very poor. There was little industry. The country was controlled by the army, the Catholic Church and the rich landowners.

Then in 1931 the Spanish King abdicated and Spain became a Republic. The people elected a left-wing government, which began to reduce the power of the Church, the army and the landowners and made plans to give land to the peasants.

In 1936 General Franco led an army rebellion against the Republican government. He was supported by the Church, the landowners and the Spanish Fascist Party. They were known as Nationalists. Franco's rebellion quickly turned into a full-scale war against the Republicans, who included peasants, factory workers and many Communists and Socialists.

Foreign countries also became involved in the Civil War. Many people in Europe and the USA believed that the Civil War was part of the growing struggle between two systems of government, dictatorship and democracy. Some supported the Nationalist rebels to stop the spread of Communism, others supported the Republicans to stop the spread of Fascism. Read Sources 1–7 and try to work out which countries got involved and why.

**SOURCE 1** From a speech by Adolf Hitler, 1936

*If Spain goes Communist, France will follow in due course, and then Germany is finished. Wedged between the Soviet bloc in the East and the French–Spanish bloc in the West, we could do nothing if Moscow chose to attack us.*

**SOURCE 2** From an account by Goering, head of the *Luftwaffe*, 1945

*With the permission of Hitler I sent transport planes and experimental fighter planes, bombers and anti-aircraft guns . . . to find out under combat conditions if they were equal to the task.*

**SOURCE 3** Count Ciano, Italian foreign minister, in 1936

*Mussolini has instructed me to tell Hitler that he will make a decisive military effort to bring about the collapse of the Republican government.*
In 1939
*Those silly people who criticised our intervention in Spain will one day perhaps understand that in the battles [in Spain] the foundations were laid for a new Roman Empire in the Mediterranean.*

**SOURCE 4** From an account by a senior Soviet official in 1941

*Moscow had a big office which did nothing else but come up with ways of disguising weapons and ammunition [bound for the Republicans]. They built freighters with false decks and tanks were immersed in the oil of tankers.*

**SOURCE 5** The American Secretary of State in 1936

*In line with well established policy this government will scrupulously refrain from any interference in the unfortunate Spanish situation.*

**SOURCE 6** From a speech by Samuel Hoare, who was in charge of the navy, to the British Cabinet in 1936

*On no account must we do anything to support Communism in Spain. It would be a grave danger to the British Empire . . . when I speak of neutrality I mean strict neutrality.*

**SOURCE 7** From the BBC television programme Timewatch, 1991

*Britain did more than merely abandon the democratically elected government in Spain. Throughout the three years of the War the British government waged a secret campaign in favour of Franco, which ensured his ultimate victory.*

1. Write the names of the following countries down one side of your page: Britain, Germany, Italy, USSR, USA.
2. Then draw three columns with the headings 'Supported Nationalists', 'Supported Republicans', 'Remained neutral'.
3. Fill in the grid to show who supported which side and any evidence about their motives which the sources provide.
4. ■ 'In the Spanish Civil War the dictatorships helped the Nationalists and the democracies helped the Republicans.' Do you agree? Explain your answer.

# Did disarmament have a chance?

ONE of the factors which caused tension between the great powers in Europe before 1914 was the race to build up great armies and navies. Because of advances in technology, weapons in 1918 were capable of killing great numbers of people; twenty million people died in the First World War.

After the War, many people wanted nations to get rid of such weapons, or at least greatly reduce them. No one wanted the same thing to happen again. This was one of the most important aims of the League of Nations. There were attempts to agree on disarmament and finally, in 1932, a Disarmament Conference was held.

Study Sources 1–8, which give the views on disarmament of the countries involved in the Conference. How likely is it that these countries will agree on disarmament? Write a report for the League of Nations.

**SOURCE 1** The view of the British government in 1926

*The British navy believes that the British Empire must have very special treatment in regard to its numbers of large warships . . . Our army is notoriously small in relation to our worldwide commitments, and it does not therefore seem capable of reduction if there is an agreement with other military powers.*

**SOURCE 2**

*The world is nowadays spending in preparing for war 600 times the sum it devotes to preparing for peace. What becomes of their sums? They are spent in men and in materials . . . While we begrudge the money we grant our schools and hospitals . . . we lavish our best material on the soldier, sailor and airman . . . costly guns, expensive aeroplanes, extravagant battleships.*

**SOURCE 3** The view of the French government at the Disarmament Conference, 1932

*Having three times suffered invasion in the last 100 years, and with long frontiers lying open to attack . . . France must have at her disposal an army and airforce powerful enough to protect herself.*

**SOURCE 4** German General Groener speaking in the German Parliament, 1931

*Germany has done her part. We have disarmed as never before seen in history. But the other powers promised to follow us along the path of disarmament. We demand they do so . . . France claims she has already done something in the way of disarmament . . . Do the thousands of tanks, aeroplanes and guns, the tens of thousands of machine guns, suggest disarmament? France also had masses of other material in store. French military expenditure had risen increasingly since the War. All these undeniable facts show that France has not begun to disarm . . . she has, perhaps, created the strongest and most effective machine of war in the world.*

**SOURCE 5** A message by President Hoover of the USA to the Disarmament Conference, 1932

*I propose the abolition of all tanks, all chemical warfare, all large mobile guns and all bombing planes . . . There should be a total ban on all bombardment from the air.*

**SOURCE 6** The view of the Soviet government, published in the newspaper Izvestia, 1932

*All the capitalist countries defended their own programmes of armaments. . . . The USA and England did not advance any special plans for reducing armaments. . . . Only the USSR presented a clear programme of disarmament.*

**SOURCE 7** From a speech by Adolf Hitler, German Chancellor, in 1933

*While the German Government again proclaims its unshaken desire for peace, it declares to its great regret that . . . it must leave the Disarmament Conference and the League of Nations.*

**SOURCE 8** From an International News Service Report, 1934

*The armaments race is on. They are off. Germany, France, Britain, Russia, Japan, Italy, are off on the race that ends in the Olympic Games of death . . . If the contest is not stopped there will be no more sense in the question 'Will war come in Europe?' The question will only be 'When will the War come?'*

# Was Britain well led between the Wars?

YOU are going to judge how well Britain tackled Europe's problems between 1919 and 1940.

> Work in pairs. Below you will find a number of problems that Britain faced. For each problem there are three possible courses of action for Britain to take.
>
> You probably remember what Britain actually did, but forget that for the time being. Imagine you are advising Britain between the Wars.
>
> For each problem, decide which of the actions would be most sensible (give that action three points) and which least sensible (give that one point). The remaining action gets two points. The first one has been done for you.

**1.** It is 1919. Germany is defeated and a peace treaty is being discussed. Should Britain:
a) agree to punish Germany *or* [2]
b) refuse to punish Germany *or* [1]
c) ask only for compensation for the damage it has suffered? [3]

**2.** It is 1919. The League of Nations, a peace-keeping organisation, is being set up. Should Britain:
a) become a member *or* ☐
b) refuse to join and isolate herself from Europe's problems *or* ☐
c) join only if the USA is a member? ☐

**3.** It is 1933. Germany is rearming and so breaking the Treaty of Versailles. Should Britain:
a) do nothing *or* ☐
b) use force to stop Germany *or* ☐
c) protest and begin to rearm herself? ☐

**4.** It is 1935. Italy is invading Abyssinia, which has appealed to the League of Nations for help. Should Britain:
a) do nothing as it wants to stay friendly with Italy *or* ☐
b) close the Suez Canal to stop Italy getting supplies to its army in Abyssinia *or* ☐
c) agree to some economic sanctions against Italy? ☐

**5.** It is 1936. Fascist Germany and the Communist USSR will both soon have the power to threaten the peace in Europe. Should Britain:
a) refuse to rearm and spend the money saved on schools and houses *or* ☐
b) begin rearming to peak in 1938 *or* ☐
c) begin rearming to peak in 1940? ☐

**6.** It is September 1938. Hitler is about to invade part of Czechoslovakia. Should Britain:
a) send troops to help the Czechs *or* ☐
b) appease Germany (i.e. give it part of Czechoslovakia, on condition that it does not invade any other countries) *or* ☐
c) leave the Czechs and Germans to sort it out between themselves? ☐

> **Scoring**
> Once you have given a score to each possible action, find out what Britain's leaders actually did in each of the situations. Add up their score according to the points you gave the possible actions.
> **6–9:** You think Britain's leaders were a failure.
> **10–13:** You think Britain's leaders did their best in a difficult situation.
> **14–18:** You think Britain had very skilful leaders.
>
> Now compare the score you have given Britain's leaders with the score that other people in the class have given them. If you disagree, find out why. Have you given the different actions different numbers of points?

# Causes of the Second World War

CUT this worksheet up to make a pack of sixteen cards.

| | |
|---|---|
| The Treaty of Versailles was too harsh on Germany | Hitler wanted Germans in Austria and Czechoslovakia to be under German rule |
| In 1939 Germany invaded Poland | France and Britain failed to stand up to Hitler early enough |
| Hitler was angry because in the 1936 Olympics held in Germany Jesse Owens, who was black, won five gold medals | Stalin took over all Soviet industry |
| In 1933 Hitler became Chancellor of Germany | People in Europe did not want another world war |

*continued* ▶

*continued* ▶

| | |
|---|---|
| In 1939 Portsmouth beat Wolves 4–1 in the FA Cup Final | Mussolini got away with invading Abyssinia |
| The USSR and Germany signed the Nazi–Soviet Pact in 1939 | The League of Nations did not have its own army |
| The USA was not interested in what was happening in Europe | Germany was defeated in the First World War |
| The world was in an economic depression between 1929 and 1933. | In 1940 Churchill became Prime Minister of Britain |

# What were the causes of the Second World War?

YOUR teacher will give you a number of 'cause' cards. Each card has on it a possible cause of the Second World War.

Work in pairs.
1. Decide which cards give sensible explanations of why the Second World War happened.
2. For each of the cards you have chosen, try to think how that cause led to the Second World War. Discuss this together.

On your own:
3. Copy the cards you have chosen into the left-hand column of the table headed 'Causes of the Second World War'.
4. In the right-hand column explain for each cause how it led to the Second World War.

**Causes of the Second World War**

| Cause | How it led to the War |
| --- | --- |
|  |  |
|  |  |
|  |  |
|  |  |
|  |  |
|  |  |
|  |  |
|  |  |
|  |  |
|  |  |
|  |  |

*continued* ▶

▶ *continued*

> **5.** In the table headed 'Other causes of the Second World War' write down any other causes of the Second World War which are not on the cards.
>
> **6.** For each other cause you have written down, explain how it led to the War.

**Other Causes of the Second World War**

| Cause | How it led to the War |
| --- | --- |
|  |  |
|  |  |
|  |  |
|  |  |
|  |  |
|  |  |
|  |  |
|  |  |
|  |  |
|  |  |
|  |  |

*continued* ▶

▶ *continued*

**7.** In the table headed 'Facts which do not explain why the Second World War happened' copy down two cause cards you have not used and state why they are not good explanations of why the War happened.

**Facts which do not explain why the Second World War happened**

| Fact | Why this did not help cause the War |
|---|---|
|  |  |
|  |  |
|  |  |
|  |  |
|  |  |
|  |  |
|  |  |
|  |  |
|  |  |
|  |  |
|  |  |
|  |  |

Now look again at the sensible explanations you chose in questions 1 and 2.

**8.** Are any of them connected? Explain the connections in your book.

**9.** Sort the cause cards into an order of importance.

**10.** Explain why the cause on the card you have put in first place is the most important.

**11.** Explain why the cause on the card you have put in last place is the least important.

# The Second World War

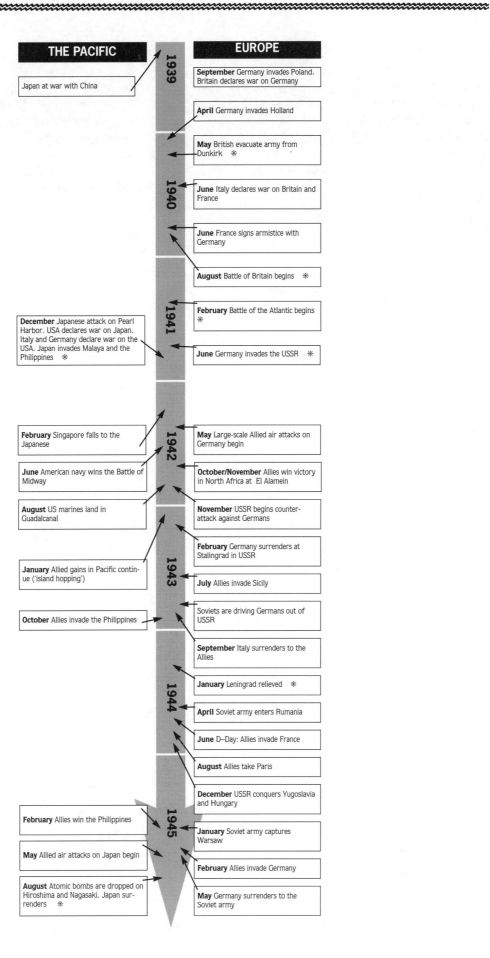

## THE PACIFIC

Japan at war with China

**December** Japanese attack on Pearl Harbor. USA declares war on Japan. Italy and Germany declare war on the USA. Japan invades Malaya and the Philippines ✶

**February** Singapore falls to the Japanese

**June** American navy wins the Battle of Midway

**August** US marines land in Guadalcanal

**January** Allied gains in Pacific continue ('island hopping')

**October** Allies invade the Philippines

**February** Allies win the Philippines

**May** Allied air attacks on Japan begin

**August** Atomic bombs are dropped on Hiroshima and Nagasaki. Japan surrenders ✶

## EUROPE

**September** Germany invades Poland. Britain declares war on Germany

**April** Germany invades Holland

**May** British evacuate army from Dunkirk ✶

**June** Italy declares war on Britain and France

**June** France signs armistice with Germany

**August** Battle of Britain begins ✶

**February** Battle of the Atlantic begins ✶

**June** Germany invades the USSR ✶

**May** Large-scale Allied air attacks on Germany begin

**October/November** Allies win victory in North Africa at El Alamein

**November** USSR begins counter-attack against Germans

**February** Germany surrenders at Stalingrad in USSR

**July** Allies invade Sicily

Soviets are driving Germans out of USSR

**September** Italy surrenders to the Allies

**January** Leningrad relieved ✶

**April** Soviet army enters Rumania

**June** D–Day: Allies invade France

**August** Allies take Paris

**December** USSR conquers Yugoslavia and Hungary

**January** Soviet army captures Warsaw

**February** Allies invade Germany

**May** Germany surrenders to the Soviet army

1939
1940
1941
1942
1943
1944
1945

# Evacuation plans

HEAVY bombing was expected in Britain's large industrial centres. The government thought that people would be safer in the country, so plans were drawn up to evacuate people from the cities.

Britain was divided into three zones:
■ evacuation areas, where heavy bombing was expected
■ reception areas – mostly country areas, safe from bombing. The evacuees would move here, and stay with local families
■ neutral areas, which might suffer light attacks. Nobody would be evacuated from or into these areas.

> **1.** On the map below, shade in where you think the evacuation areas, reception areas and neutral areas were.

> **2.** About thirteen million people lived in the evacuation areas. But there was room in the reception areas for just 4.8 million people. The government said that certain groups of people should be moved first. Which groups of people would you have moved first?

---

**Evacuation: priority groups**

First priority ...........................................

Second priority .......................................

Third priority ........................................

---

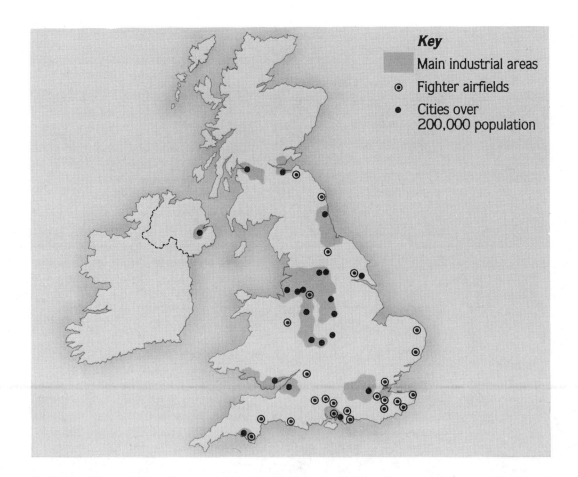

**Key**

▨ Main industrial areas

◉ Fighter airfields

● Cities over 200,000 population

**SOURCE 1** Industrial areas and centres of population

**PEACE & WAR** THE TWENTIETH-CENTURY WORLD

# Carrie's War

THESE extracts come from a novel called *Carrie's War* by Nina Bawden, first published in 1975

*'Oh, it'll be such fun,' their mother had said when she kissed them goodbye at the station. 'Living in the country instead of the stuffy old city. You'll love it, you see if you don't!' As if Hitler had arranged this old war for their benefit, just so that Carrie and Nick could be sent away in a train with gas masks slung over their shoulders and their names on cards round their necks. Labelled like parcels – Caroline Wendy Willow and Nicholas Peter Willow – only with no address to be sent to. None of them, not even the teachers, knew where they were going. 'That's part of the adventure,' Carrie's mother had said, and not just to cheer them up: it was her nature to look on the bright side. If she found herself in Hell, Carrie thought now, she'd just say, 'Well, at least we'll be warm.'*

*Thinking of her mother, always making the best of things (or pretending to: when the train began to move she had stopped smiling) Carrie nearly did cry. There was a lump like a pill stuck in her throat. She swallowed hard and pulled faces.*

*The train was slowing. 'Here we are,' Miss Fazackerly said. 'Collect your things, don't leave anything. Take care of Nick, Carrie.' . . .*

*Nick clung to Carrie's sleeve as they went through the door into a long, dark room with pointed windows. It was crowded and noisy. Someone said to Carrie, 'Would you like a cup of tea,. bach? And a bit of cake, now?' She was a cheerful, plump woman with a sing-song Welsh voice. Carrie shook her head; she felt cake would choke her. 'Stand by there, then,' the woman said. 'There by the wall with the others, and someone will choose you.'*

*Carrie looked round, bewildered, and saw Albert Sandwich. She whispered, 'What's happening?' and he said, 'A kind of cattle auction, it seems.' . . .*

*Carrie had already begun to feel ill with shame and fear that no one would choose her, the way she always felt when they picked teams at school. Suppose she was left to the last! She dragged Nick into the line of waiting children and stood, eyes on the ground, hardly daring to breathe. When someone called out, 'A nice little girl for Mrs Davies, now,' she felt she would suffocate. She looked up but unfocused her eyes so that passing faces blurred and swam in front of her.*

*Nick's hand tightened in hers. She looked at his white face and the traces of sick round his mouth and wanted to shake him. No one would take home a boy who looked like that, so pale and delicate. They would think he was bound to get ill and be a trouble to them. She said in a low, fierce voice, 'Why don't you smile and look nice,' and he blinked with surprise, looking so small and so sweet that she softened. She said, 'Oh it's all right, I'm not cross. I won't leave you.'*

*Minutes passed, feeling like hours. Children left the line and were taken away. Only unwanted ones left . . .*

*Someone had stopped in front of her. Someone said, 'Surely you can take two, Mrs Evans?'*

*'Two girls, perhaps. Not a boy and a girl, I'm afraid. I've only the one room, see, and my brother's particular.'*

*Particular about what, Carrie wondered. But Mrs Evans looked nice; a little like a red squirrel Carrie had once seen, peering round a tree in a park. Reddish brown hair and bright, button eyes, and a shy, quivering look.*

*Carrie said, 'Nick sleeps in my room at home because he has bad dreams sometimes. I always look after him and he's no trouble at all.'*

*Mrs Evans looked doubtful. 'Well, I don't know what my brother will say. Perhaps I can chance it.' She smiled at Carrie.*

1. Can you find any evidence in these extracts that the author has researched the period, or is the story completely made up?
a) Mark some parts which have been researched. You will find it useful to have another look at pages 154–157 of your textbook.
b) Mark some parts where the author has used her imagination to convey what people were feeling.
2. Do you think the parts where the author has used her imagination have any value to someone studying evacuation, or are they just there to make the story more interesting?
3. This book is fiction. It has been written to entertain people. How has this had an effect on the way the author has written the story?
4. Do you think that overall these extracts give a realistic idea of what evacuation was like?

# How has the War changed your life?

EACH of these characters has been asked: 'How has the War changed your life?' What will they say? Fill in the speech bubbles to show how each person might answer.

# Convoy

THIS map shows the situation in the Atlantic in January–June 1942.

You have to make plans for ten merchant ships to sail from New York to Southampton. You have been told that that you have an escort for only half of your journey.

1. Write notes about:
   - which parts of the journey will be the most dangerous
   - where you will use the escorts
   - which parts of the Atlantic you want to keep away from
   - how you will organise the ten ships. Will they travel in one large convoy, or will you send them out individually?
   - what you fear the most: U-boats, warships, mines, aircraft, merchant raiders, or E-boats (torpedo boats)
   - what else you can do to help make the journey as safe as possible.

2. Mark your chosen route on the map, with notes which include all the points mentioned above, e.g. showing areas of greatest danger.

Key

∴∴∴   Allied merchant ships sunk Jan–July 1942

▨   Limit of Allied air cover

ICELAND

BRITAIN

Southampton

EUROPE

AFRICA

CANADA

New York

USA

SOUTH AMERICA

N

0   1000 km

# A comic war!

THESE are extracts from a comic strip set in the Second World War. The story takes place in Italy early in 1944. Fierce fighting is going on between the German army and the Allies. The Germans are in retreat, but a German SS Officer, Karl Groesz, and a band of Italian Fascists have captured some British ambulances and converted them into armoured cars. They plan to use them to attack an arms store behind Allied lines and capture much-needed ammunition and weapons.

Corporal Bill Smith and Captain Adam Philip have realised what Groesz is up to, but their superior officers will not listen to them. They decide to go to the arms store and warn the guards.

Then Bill notices movements in the hills . . .

**SOURCE 1** Frames from *Commando*, a comic published since the War

*continued* ▶

# WORKSHEET 42

▶ continued

THE FASCISTS OPENED UP THROUGH HOLES CUT IN THE AMBULANCES ON THE SHERMAN THAT THREATENED TO BLOCK THEIR WAY.

KEEP FIRING — IT'S OUR ONLY CHANCE!

IT'S NO GOOD, THE BULLETS JUST BOUNCE OFF.

THE TANK HIT THE LEAD AMBULANCE WITH A SAVAGE CRUNCH.

GOT HIM!

AGH!

BILL DIDN'T STOP THERE. HE USED THE REMORSELESS PRESSURE OF THE TANK'S ENGINES TO SLEW THE FIRST VEHICLE ACROSS THE ROAD FOR THE OTHERS TO CRASH INTO.

AAGH!

WOW, WHAT A PILE-UP!

1. Fill in the empty word bubbles in the sixth frame. Your teacher will tell you what the cartoonist wrote.
2. Complete the story by drawing two frames in the empty squares. Write captions for the squares.
3. Do you think the main purpose of the cartoon is
a) to teach people about the Second World War
b) to tell an exciting story
c) to show that war and violence are bad? Give reasons for your answer.
4. How has the purpose of the cartoonist affected what he has drawn and how he has drawn it?
5. Is there any evidence that anything in the story was based on research?
6. Choose three parts of the story which you think have been made up.
7. How realistic do you think the story is about what life was like during the Second World War?

# How did other countries react to the persecution of the Jews?

SOURCES 1–5 summarise international reactions to the persecution of the Jews during the 1930s and 1940s. As you read through these sources, you should keep two questions in mind:

■ How much did other countries know about what was happening to the Jews?
■ How much help did the Jews get from other countries?

## The 1930s

Reports of Hitler's anti-Jewish policies were published in British and American newspapers soon after he came to power in 1933. Source 1 shows the attitude of the American government in 1933.

---

**SOURCE 1** A statement by the American State Department, 1933

*Unfortunate incidents have indeed been taking place, and the whole world joins in regretting them. But without minimising or agreeing with what has taken place, I have reason to believe that many of the accounts of terror and atrocities which have reached this country have been exaggerated, and I fear that to continue to spread exaggerated reports may harm the friendly feelings between the peoples of the two countries and be of doubtful service to anyone.*

---

**SOURCE 2** Written by the historian Tony Bayfield about the attitude of other countries in his book *Churban: Jewish Responses* in 1981

*A discreet silence [on the Jewish question] was the order of the day.*

*Certainly, other countries had their own problems in the 1930s – slump, depression, unemployment.*

*The American politician Hamilton Fish said: 'It is of no concern to America what form of government is set up in Germany or in any other nation.'*

---

During the 1930s Nazi persecution of Jews grew worse. At the same time the Nazi government was preparing to stage the 1936 Olympic Games in Berlin. Propaganda Minister Goering made sure that the world saw the official image of a successful Germany recovering from the Depression. *Der Stürmer*, the anti-Jewish magazine, was removed from the news-stands during the Olympics. Foreign journalists were taken to expensive parties. They were not allowed near concentration camps or ghettoes. When the Games were over *Der Stürmer* returned and the Nazis carried on as before.

The persecution of the Jews was reported in British newspapers, as Source 3 shows. This article reveals the attitude of at least some people in Britain towards Jews.

---

**SOURCE 3** From an article in the *Sunday Express*, June 1938

*Inside Germany the Jews are being herded from one place to another in Black Marias [police vans]. They are driven to and fro, threatened and insulted . . . And although no actual violence has been shown them in the present outbreak, the Jews are sore afraid . . .*

*The Jews are being persecuted in Germany because they have become too prosperous in the German state . . . Half the lawyers and half the doctors in Germany were Jews. The persecution of Jews always follows the prosperity of the Jews . . .*

*In Britain half a million Jews find their home . . . They are never persecuted and, indeed, in many respects the Jews are given favoured treatment here.*

*But just now there is a big influx of foreign Jews into Britain. They are over-running the country. They are trying to enter the medical profession in great numbers. They wish to practise as dentists.*

*The hostility to the Jews in Germany cannot be condoned. But beware lest the present rush of Jews into this country injures the cause of Jewry here . . . For professional men naturally resent their livings being taken from them by immigrants from foreign countries, whether they be Jew or Gentile . . .*

*There is no intolerance in Britain today. Intolerance is loathed and hated by almost everybody in this country. And by keeping a close watch on the causes which fed the intolerance of the Jews in other European countries we shall be able to continue to treat well those Jews who have made their homes among us, many of them for generations.*

---

1. Read Source 3. Choose five phrases which show British attitudes towards the Jews.
2. How would you sum up what this source tells you about British attitudes towards Jews?

---

▶ *continued*

▶ *continued*

## During the War

In September 1939 the German army entered Warsaw. The Jews were gathered together and herded into a walled off part of the city, which became known as the ghetto. This process was repeated in other Eastern European cities captured by the Germans.

A Jew called Shmuel Zygielboym escaped to the West and warned ambassadors, journalists, government officials and anyone else who would listen about the terrible things which were being done to the Jews in the lands occupied by the Germans.

In April 1943 an international conference was held in Bermuda to discuss the alarming information about the Jews. The conference decided that no refuge or help could be offered to the Jews.

> **SOURCE 4** From a speech by the American Secretary of State at the Bermuda Conference, 1943
>
> 66 *The unknown cost of moving an unknown number of persons from an unknown place to an unknown destination, a scheme advocated by certain pressure groups, is of course out of the question.* 99

In June 1944 the Americans received a report from two Jews who had escaped from Auschwitz. The report included detailed plans of the gas chambers. The American War Department refused to bomb railway lines between Hungary and Auschwitz because it would 'divert air support from the decisive operations'. The War Department said that armed force would not be used for rescuing victims of enemy persecution unless the rescues were carried out with the aim of defeating enemy forces. A request to bomb gas chambers was turned down.

After May 1944 the American airforce had bases in Italy. American planes had the range and the bombs to cut the rail routes to the gas chambers. On 7 July 1944, 452 bombers flew over two of the railway lines leading to Auschwitz. Their orders were to bomb the nearby oil installations, but not the camp.

Six hundred thousand Jews were transported from Hungary to Auschwitz between March and July 1944. The killings continued right up to the end of the War, and Hitler used railway lines and trains for the Holocaust rather than for the war effort, where they were badly needed. Even in his last will and testament Hitler urged Germans to continue the fight against the Jews.

When Allied soldiers reached the camps they found piles of recently gassed bodies which the SS had not had time to bury.

> **SOURCE 5** From *The People's War* by Angus Calder
>
> 66 *In January 1942, leading British newspapers reported that over a million Jews had been killed since the outbreak of war. Word of the extermination of Jewish prisoners with a new gas, Zyklon B, had soon reached Britain.*
>
> *But . . . when the Archbishop of Canterbury described the treatment of the Jews as 'the most appalling horror in recorded history', and when the government minister Eden spoke of 'barbarous and inhuman treatment', they were using words which no longer had any force. The atrocity stories which had churned out of the propaganda machines of both sides in the First World War, and which had seemed ridiculous soon after it had ended, had made intelligent people extremely sceptical. So when they heard about Zyklon B and the reduction of human beings to soap, they only half believed in them.* 99

3. Collect together the evidence you can find to support each of the following statements for a) before the War, and b) during the War:
   - 'The international community knew nothing about the persecution of the Jews.'
   - 'The international community was unsympathetic to the problems of the Jews.'
4. Which of the statements best describes the situation before and during the War?
5. Do you agree with the decision by the American government that the most important aim was to defeat Germany and that nothing should be done which would slow this up? Or do you think the transport links to the camps, or even the camps themselves, should have been bombed?
6. In pairs, look back through all the evidence about the Holocaust on this worksheet and in your textbook on pages 186–193.
   a) Make a list of the different groups of people who should take some of the responsibility for the Holocaust.
   b) Explain why each of these groups was in some way responsible.

# **W**hy do accounts of the past disagree?

THE chart below gives some reasons why accounts of the past disagree. Use this to help you investigate contradictions between sources. You can probably add other reasons for disagreement in the empty boxes.

| | | |
|---|---|---|
| When it was written | Different political ideas | Use of different statistics |
| Gaps in evidence | Different historians use different sources | Different ideas |
| Different race | Different gender | |
| Different nationality | | |

# The war in Europe

THESE events from the Second World War in Europe are in the wrong order.

1. Cut up the page to make eight 'event cards'.
2. Without looking up the dates of any of the events, place them in the order you think is correct and explain why you think they must have happened in that order.
3. Now look in your textbook to check the date of each event and see if you have got them all in the correct order.
4. Choose any two events which you think helped the Allies win the Second World War. Explain why you think they are important.

| | |
|---|---|
| Germany invades Poland | D-Day landings: Allies invade France |
| Hitler commits suicide | Soviet army reaches Berlin |
| Germans take Paris | Germany invades USSR |
| Allies land in Sicily and then invade Italy | Britain and France declare war on Germany |

▶ continued

▶ *continued*

| | |
|---|---|
| Churchill replaces Chamberlain as Prime Minister | Germany conquers Belgium |
| Battle of Britain won by RAF, German invasion of Britain postponed | Germany declares war on USA |
| British and Allied troops evacuated from Dunkirk and saved from advancing German army | Germans surrender at Stalingrad |
| Germany and USSR sign Nazi–Soviet Pact | USSR invades Rumania |
| Allies take Paris | German army surrenders |

5. Cut out the ten cards on this page.
6. Add these to the first eight in the correct order. Check your answer with your teacher or in a reference book.
7. Choose four events which strengthened Germany's position in the War. Explain how each did this.
8. Choose four events which helped the Allies to win the War. Explain how each one helped.
9. Which event in your last list was the most important? Explain why.
10. Decide at what dates you would say: a) Germany was at the peak of her powers in Europe, b) the tide began to turn against Germany, c) the Allies were bound to win.

# **W**hy were the atomic bombs dropped?

LOOK at Sources 8–20 on pages 200–201 of your textbook. What evidence can you find for or against each of the four views shown on this chart? Write your evidence down in the columns provided.

| American casualties would be heavy if the USA did not drop the bomb | | The USA wanted to test its expensive new weapon | |
|---|---|---|---|
| Evidence for | Evidence against | Evidence for | Evidence against |
|  |  |  |  |

| The USA wanted the USSR to see how powerful it was | | The USA wanted to teach the Japanese a lesson | |
|---|---|---|---|
| Evidence for | Evidence against | Evidence for | Evidence against |
|  |  |  |  |

# War crimes

THE question of whether people should be tried for committing 'war crimes' is a difficult one. For example:
- Should only those on the losing side be charged?
- War by its very nature involves dreadful things being done. How can we decide which ones are so dreadful that they are not justified even by war?
- Should soldiers be found guilty of war crimes if they were obeying orders?
- Should individuals be found guilty, or whole nations?

On 20 November 1945, the trial of 24 leading Nazis started at Nuremberg. There were four charges:
- crimes against peace: carrying out wars of aggression
- war crimes: ill-treatment of prisoners of war and civilians
- crimes against humanity: extreme brutality against whole groups of people
- conspiracy: plotting together to commit these crimes.

Some of the men on trial were leading Nazis, members of Hitler's government like Goering and Speer. Some were men who were in charge of the camps, such as Hoss, the commandant of Auschwitz. Twelve were sentenced to death by hanging, others were acquitted, and some were imprisoned.

These were the views of some British people at the time:
- 'They should have been put against the wall and shot.' (A secretary)
- 'I think we have missed a great opportunity to show that we are more civilised than the Germans. We could have kept them in detention and given them an opportunity to work out their salvation or forever remain prisoners.' (A businessman)
- 'It is the men who ran the camps who should be hanged. I think Goering and the rest were just doing their duty and did not know much of what went on in these places.' (A Polish pilot who flew with the RAF, and was a prisoner of war for three years)

1. Based on all you have so far studied about the Second World War, you have to decide the most appropriate verdict for each of the following:
- Hitler
- a member of the SS *Einsatzgruppe*, acting under orders (Source 13 on page 189)
- Rudolf Hoss, commandant of Auschwitz (Source 19 on page 191)
- Admiral Donitz, head of the German navy and responsible for the U-boat campaign in the Atlantic (pages 176–179).

Possible verdicts are guilty, not guilty, or not proven.

Possible sentences are execution, imprisonment, or to be let free.

Remember that dreadful things happen in all wars. Discuss in class what kinds of things are so dreadful that they cannot be allowed even in a time of war.

2. Some people on the Allied side are sometimes criticised for what they did. What verdict would you pass on:
- 'Bomber' Harris (pages 194–197)
- Prime Minister Churchill
- the pilots who flew the plane which dropped the atomic bombs on Japan (pages 198–201)
- President Truman, who ordered the dropping of the bombs?

3. Copy the chart below and fill it in, adding your reasons for each decision.

|  | Verdict | Sentence | Reasons |
|---|---|---|---|
| Hitler |  |  |  |
| *Einsatzgruppe* soldier |  |  |  |
| Hoss |  |  |  |
| Admiral Donitz |  |  |  |
| 'Bomber' Harris |  |  |  |
| Churchill |  |  |  |
| pilots |  |  |  |
| Truman |  |  |  |

# The new Europe

SOURCES 1–3 are maps of Europe. The first is completed to show the borders before the Great War in 1914.

1. Complete Sources 2 and 3 to show the situation in 1919 and 1945. You will need to consult Source 2 on page 117 and Source 7 on page 210 of your textbook.
2. Write three paragraphs to explain what the main changes were.

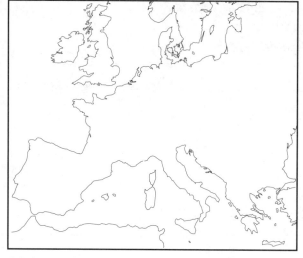

**SOURCE 2**

**SOURCE 1**

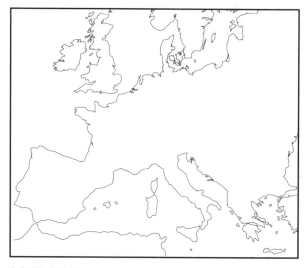

**SOURCE 3**

# Discovering the Past in Key Stage 3

## Y7

| | | |
|---|---|---|
| **Contrasts and Connections** | Pupils' Book | 0 7195 4938 8 |
| | Teachers' Resource Book, 2nd edn | 0 7195 7040 9 |
| **Discovering The Roman Empire** | Pupils' Book | 0 7195 5179 X |
| | Teachers' Evaluation Pack | 0 7195 5180 3 |
| **Discovering Medieval Realms** | Pupils' Book | 0 7195 5177 3 |
| | Teachers' Evaluation Pack | 0 7195 5178 1 |
| **Medieval Realms Special Needs Support Materials** | Picture Pack | 0 7195 5382 2 |
| | Picture Pack Workbook | 0 7195 7056 5 |
| | Teachers' Resource Book | 0 7195 4979 5 |
| **Castles and Cathedrals** | Pupils' Book | 0 7195 4952 3 |
| | Teachers' Evaluation Pack | 0 7195 4979 5 |

## Y8

| | | |
|---|---|---|
| **Societies in Change** | Pupils' Book | 0 7195 4975 2 |
| | Teachers' Resource Book, 2nd edn | 0 7195 7041 7 |
| **Discovering The Making of the UK** | Pupils' Book | 0 7195 7052 2 |
| | Teachers' Evaluation Pack | 0 7195 7053 0 |
| **The Making of the UK Special Needs Support Materials** | Picture Pack | 0 7195 7044 1 |
| | Picture Pack Workbook | 0 7195 7226 6 |
| | Teachers' Resource Book | 0 7195 7043 3 |
| **The Renaissance** | Pupils' Book | 0 7195 5186 2 |
| | Teachers' Evaluation Pack | 0 7195 5187 0 |

## Y9

| | | |
|---|---|---|
| **Peace and War** | Pupils' Book | 0 7195 4977 9 |
| | Teachers' Resource Book | 0 7195 4978 7 |
| **Britain 1750–1900 Special Needs Support Materials** | Picture Pack | 0 7195 7046 8 |
| | Picture Pack Workbook | 0 7195 7227 4 |
| | Teachers' Resource Book | 0 7195 7045 X |
| **The Twentieth-Century World – Special Needs Support Materials** | Picture Pack | 0 7195 7048 4 |
| | Picture Pack Workbook | 0 7195 7228 2 |
| | Teachers' Resource Book | 0 7195 7047 6 |
| **Britain and the Great War** | Pupils' Book | 0 7195 5148 X |
| | Teachers' Evaluation Pack | 0 7195 5152 8 |
| **The Changing Role of Women** | Pupils' Book | 0 7195 5106 4 |
| | Teachers' Evaluation Pack | 0 7195 5107 2 |

Available from John Murray, 50 Albemarle Street, London W1X 4BD